REA

KINKY FRIEDMAN

YOU CAN LEAD A POLITICIAN TO WATER, BUT YOU CAN'T MAKE HIM THINK

TEN COMMANDMENTS FOR TEXAS POLITICS

SIMON & SCHUSTER
NEW YORK   LONDON   TORONTO   SYDNEY

Simon & Schuster
1230 Avenue of the Americas
New York, NY 10020

First Simon & Schuster hardcover edition October 2007

SIMON & SCHUSTER and colophon are registered trademarks of Simon &
Schuster, Inc.

For information regarding special discounts for bulk purchases,
please contact Simon & Schuster Special Sales at
1-800-456-6798 or business@simonandschuster.com

Designed by Karolina Harris

Manufactured in the United States of America

10   9   8   7   6   5   4   3   2   1

Library of Congress Cataloging-in-Publication Data
Friedman, Kinky.
You can lead a politician to water, but you can't make him think : ten command-
ments for Texas politics / Kinky Friedman.
    p. cm.
1. Texas—Politics and government—1951 2. Political campaigns—Texas.
3. Elections—Texas. 4. Governors—Texas—Election. 5. Politics, Practical—Texas.
I. Title.
JK4816.F75 2007
324.9764'064—dc22   2007009572
ISBN-13: 978-1-4165-4760-0
ISBN-10:   1-4165-4760-6

This book is dedicated to the 170,258 Texans, four times the number required by law, who stayed out of the primaries in order to sign our petition to get on the ballot. This archaic law, forcing people who wish to support an independent candidate not to vote in the primaries, is part of the reason no independent has gotten on the ballot for governor since Sam Houston a hundred and fifty years ago.

Thanks to you folks, the "Save Yourself for Kinky" campaign was a big success and modern Texas history was written.

I dedicate this book to every one of you, including the memory of Lucille O'Brien from Breckinridge, who saved herself for Kinky, signing the petition on her 100th birthday.

CONTENTS

Contents

Contents

"The people have spoken—the bastards!"

—*Dick Tuck, legendary political dirty trickster*

YOU CAN LEAD A POLITICIAN TO WATER, BUT YOU CAN'T MAKE HIM THINK

The Jewish Zorro? Nope. The artwork of the great Guy Juke.
(Art by Guy Juke)

A PREFACE

Well, folks, it was fun being the governor-in-waiting. By this writing, however, the votes have been cast and counted and the race has been run and I am still not the governor. I gave Texas my telephone number and she never got back to me. I admit to being a little disappointed but I'm not downhearted. Remember, the crowd picked Barabbas.

Now before you get started, let me just say that

I'm not comparing myself to Jesus, nor am I comparing any particular politician to Barabbas. I'm merely pointing out that the crowd had a choice and their choice was to let Jesus die and to let Barabbas go. Now two thousand years have passed and we haven't heard a hell of a lot from Barabbas. He doesn't call, he doesn't write, he hasn't saved a single soul. On the other hand, Jesus has saved millions of people, and, if anyone can do it, he may just be our last best chance of saving the world, not to mention winning an ungodly number of football games. So you see, the crowd does not always make the best choice. It is possible to lose the election, but win the war. This is done with spirit and heart and guts and perseverance. I am now free at last, free to wander in the raw poetry of time. I will continue, nonetheless, to endeavor to be a dealer in hope, hope for a better, brighter future for Texas. And hope is what we need now more than ever. The way things are going, the only two choices we'll soon have will be flour or corn.

I once said, "I'll sign anything but bad legislation." This is still true; it's just a little harder for me to stop the bad legislation that's affecting all of our lives. With bad legislation and a pathetic lack of good leadership, Texas will always find herself following, never leading the American parade. That's one reason I wrote this book; another is, I needed the bucks. Hey, Jewish cowboy speaks the truth. And the truth is, I love Texas and I hate what the politicians are doing to her.

How did I get into this mess in the first place?

Read on, gentile reader, read on. For this is not simply a book about a campaign or even a spiritual quest. It is a search for that beautiful place that is above politics—a place, I believe, that can only be found if we look together.

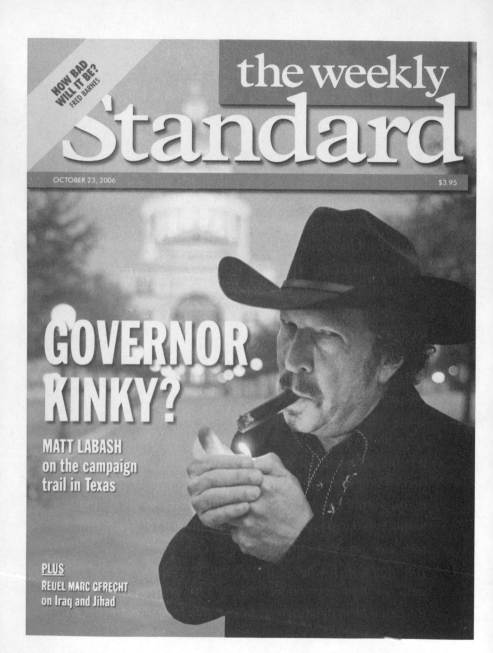

We won the race every place but Texas!
(Courtesy of The Weekly Standard*)*

AN
INTRODUCTION:
OLD
TESTAMENTS
AND NEW
REVELATIONS

OAF OF OFFICE

As the only man who's slept at the White House under two presidents, Bill Clinton and George W. Bush, it was probably only a matter of time before I jumped into politics myself. At the White House early in 2003, as I was advising Bush on Iraq, I thought I heard him mention putting me in charge of the National Park Service. It's about time he appointed a real cowboy, I said to myself as I adjusted my fanny pack. I knew, of course, that this would not be a cabinet-level appointment. I would probably have a portfolio of some kind, a small staff of busy little bureaucrats to do all the work, and I'd no doubt carry the title of undersecretary. That was fine with me. I'd probably be spending most of my time under my secretary anyway.

As I left the East Wing, I became more and more certain that, if not exactly offering me a position, the president was subtly encouraging me to get back into politics. I'd been on hiatus since my unsuccessful campaign for justice of the peace in Kerrville in 1986, in which my slogan was "If you elect me the first Jewish justice of the peace, I'll reduce the speed limits to 54.95." But that was then and this was now. So, I waited in the full-crouch position for a call from someone in the administration. When it didn't come, I couldn't decide whether to kill myself or get a haircut.

There must be a place in politics for a man of my talents, I thought. Dogcatcher might be a good place to start. I could free all the dogs and encourage them to lay some serious cable in the yards of people I didn't like. Or maybe I could run for mayor of Austin. I could fight against the fascist anti-smoking laws. I probably couldn't win without appealing to all the techno geeks, but a good slogan would help—something like "A cigar in every mouth and a chip on every shoulder" might work. Basically, though, it'd be too small a gig for the Kinkster. I had bigger fish to fry.

Well, I thought, what about governor of Texas? That might be therapeutic. It's a notoriously easy gig, and I'd certainly be the most colorful candidate since Pappy O'Daniel. Hell, compared with most politicians, I'm practically Mr. Charismo. I can work a room better than anyone since the late John Tower went to that great caucus in the sky. When I meet a potential voter, I'm good for precisely three minutes of superficial charm. If I stay for five minutes, I can almost see the pity in the person's eyes.

Nevertheless, being governor might be a lot of fun. I've known the last two and a half governors, and they didn't seem to be working all that hard. Of course, I saw them mostly at social events. In fact, I once mistook Rick Perry for a wine steward at the Governor's Mansion. I said, "Hey, you look familiar. Do I know you?" And he said, "Yeah. I'm the governor, Rick Perry." Then he gave me a friendly handshake and looked at me like he was trying to establish eye contact with a unicorn. He didn't seem as funny as Ann Richards or George W., but he came off like a pretty nice guy for an Aggie.

After some minor soul-searching, I decided to throw my ten-gallon yarmulke in the ring and form an exploratory committee headed by the dead Dutch explorer Sir Wilhelm Rumphumper. The committee had one meeting and came back with the consensus that, as long as Willie Nelson or Pat Green didn't decide to run, I could be the next governor. They offered the opinion that many of Pat's people were probably too young to vote and that

KINKY FRIEDMAN

Willie, God bless him, did not quite present as clean-cut an image as I did. Also, neither of them had had any previous experience in politics. Not only had I run for justice of the peace, but I'd also been chairman of the Gay Texans for Phil Gramm committee.

Though the report was encouraging, I had to admit that I was beginning to find the prospect of the governorship rather limiting. I aspired to inspire before I expired. There had to be something I could do for my country besides flying five American flags from my pickup truck and telling the guy with four American flags on his pickup truck to "Go back to Afghanistan, you communist bastard!" But what of the president's offer? To clear the boards for my race for governor, I asked my old Austin High pal Billy Gammon to check the status of my appointment. Billy's so close to the president he gets to fly in the White House helicopter. "I stand ready to serve!" I told Billy.

"I'll get back to you," he said.

And he did. He told me that while the Bushes obviously considered the Kinkster a dear friend, the president had only been engaging in light banter when he'd raised the possibility of my moving into public housing. Billy also said that though I might have made a "fantastic contribution to government," George W. could see how I also might well have been a "scandal waiting to happen."

"That's good news," I told Billy, "because I'm running for governor and I'd like you to be my campaign manager."

"I'll get back to you," he said.

I got over my disappointment quickly. Like most of us, I'd determined that I'd rather be a large part of the problem than a small part of the solution. Besides, I had Big Mo on my side. I wasn't sure how traveling with a large homosexual would go down with the voters, but hell, I'd try anything. Just recently, for instance, I tried making a campaign pitch to my fellow passengers on a crowded elevator. After several of them threatened to call 911, however, it unfortunately put me a little off-message. "Now that I have you people all together," I told them, "I can't remember what I wanted you for."

SEE KINKY RUN

There were yet to be, however, a number of interesting developments, and not all of them transpiring entirely within the febrile confines of my gray-matter department. There actually *did* seem to be genuine support for my candidacy. A good bit of it, unfortunately, appeared to be emanating from the Bandera Home for the Bewildered.

In Washington, late in 2003, the president himself promised me that if I ran for governor, he would be my "one-man focus group." During the same White House visit, I had a cordial meeting in a hallway with Colin Powell and later found myself in the men's room with Donald Rumsfeld. Though neither man offered to help with my campaign, I did mention to Rummy that he was not the most famous person I'd ever wee-wee-wee'd next to. The most famous, I told him, was Groucho Marx. Rummy told me he couldn't touch that one but that his wife had once danced with Jimmy Durante.

A few weeks later, at the Texas Book Festival, my campaign won the support of Molly Ivins, the late, legendary journalist I sometimes refer to as the conscience of Texas. She asked me point-blank why I was running. "Why the hell not?" I replied. "Beautiful," she said. "That's your campaign slogan." Any candidate for governor of Texas who has the support of both George W. and Molly can't be all bad.

Texas, as Molly pointed out, has a tradition of singing governors. I thought back to Pappy O'Daniel's successful race for that esteemed office in the 1940s. He had a band called the Light Crust Doughboys. I had a band called the Texas Jewboys. His slogan was "Pass the biscuits, Pappy." One of my most popular songs is "Get Your Biscuits in the Oven (And Your Buns in the Bed)." The parallels are uncanny.

Thus, with George and Molly aboard, I felt empowered enough to do an interview with the *Kerrville Daily Times*, break the news to my friend U.S. congressman Lamar Smith, and green-light a first printing of bumper stickers that read "He Ain't Kinky. He's My Governor." (These were quickly followed by my pal Harley Belew's idea: "My Governor Is a Jewish Cowboy.") The Kerrville paper trumpeted my interview on page one, the bumper stickers proliferated throughout the Hill Country faster than jackrabbits, and Lamar suggested that the race, quixotic as it might seem, would be a no-lose proposition. "You'll come out of this," he predicted, "with a book, a wife, or the governorship." I don't want a wife, I told him. I'm already married to Texas. He was right about the book, of course. As far as winning the governorship is concerned, I now suspect widespread voter fraud. It had to be. Everyone I meet claims he voted for me.

It was around this time that some people began asking me if the whole thing was a joke. For some reason this rankled me more than I'd expected. I'd always seen myself, in the words of Billy Joe Shaver, as a serious soul nobody took seriously. Why should they take me seriously now? But I wasn't ready to retire in a petulant snit to a goat farm for sixteen years. I'd tell them the truth with humor, for humor always sails dangerously close to the truth. Some things are too important to be taken seriously, I told them. The question, I added, is whether my candidacy is a joke or whether the current crop of politicians is the joke.

But there was a time in late November 2004 when I didn't have such a positive attitude. I paced back and forth in my log cabin, wondering if I was bound for the Governor's Mansion or the mental hospital. I was so uncertain of my chances at that dark time that if I'd been elected, I would have demanded a recount. Did I dare dream the impossible dream? Go for the long shot? Then the phone rang. The caller said he was from the *Times*. "That was some interview you guys did," I said. "What interview?" asked the guy. "Isn't this the *Kerrville Daily Times*?" I asked. "No," he said. "It's the *New York Times.*"

The *Times* story, written by Ralph Blumenthal, headlined "Guess Who Wants to Be Governor," ran on Saturday, November 29, a day that will live in infamy in the minds of those who wish to perpetuate the politics of the status quo. The switchboard at the ranch lit up like a Christmas tree in Las Vegas. Fielding the congratulatory calls and the offers of support was a daunting task, but I tried to be as gracious as possible. I told them all I'd get back to them in about two years.

But the calls kept coming. My old pal Tom Waits offered to come down and help the campaign, as did Willie Nelson, Dwight Yoakam, Robert Duvall, Billy Bob Thornton, Jim Nabors, Jerry Jeff Walker, Lily Tomlin, and Johnny Depp. In addition to this galaxy of stars, Penn and Teller, the Las Vegas magicians, promised to come to Texas and "make the opposition disappear." Meanwhile, Craven and Nancy Green, the parents of a struggling young songwriter named Pat Green, came up to the ranch from Waco. They brought with them the Sunday *Waco Tribune-Herald*, which had carried the *New York Times* story. "It's on page one," they said excitedly, but they seemed a bit hesitant to show me. After some badgering, I got them to hand me the paper. The story was there all right, but the Waco editors had changed the headline to read "Uncouth Hopeful Eyes Governorship." The campaign was already getting personal.

So what kind of governor would I be? When I was in

Washington, George W. asked me what my platform was. I didn't really have an answer at the time, but I'd had a chance to think it over. Next time I saw him, I vowed, this would be what I'd say: "My platform, Mr. President, is that I'm not a politician. My platform is that I'm not a bureaucrat. My platform is that I'm a writer of fiction who speaks the truth. My platform is to fight the wussification of this great state, to rise and shine and bring back the glory of Texas. My platform is no hill to a climber. My platform is to remember that when they went out searching for Sam Houston to try to persuade him to be the governor—and he was the greatest governor this state has ever had—rumor has it that they found him drunk, sleeping under a bridge with the Indians."

On second thought, I've finally realized, maybe I didn't really want a platform. They'd probably try to put a trapdoor in it.

DOME IMPROVEMENT

There once was a zoo that some folks liked to call Texas politics. In this zoo were hawks and doves, bulls and bears, crocodiles and two-legged snakes, and lots and lots and lots of sheep. But the ones who ran the zoo were not really animals. They were people dressed up in elephant and donkey suits who'd lined their pockets long ago and now went around lying to everybody and making all the rules. Even as a child, I knew I never wanted to be one of

Speaking at the Texas Senate—a building built for giants but inhabited by midgets.
(Photo by Brian Kanof)

them, a constipated, humorless, perfunctory, political party hack. This did not stop me, of course, from growing up to be a party animal.

Unless you've been living in a double-wide deer blind, you know I ran for governor in 2006. Actually, being a rather indecisive person, I almost didn't run. I had to weigh the impact the race might have on my family. You might be thinking, "The Kinkster doesn't have a family." But that's not quite right, folks: Texas is my family.

By running as an independent, I hoped to demonstrate that even if the governor doesn't really do any heavy lifting, he can still do some spiritual lifting. There's a place above politics that has nothing to do with bureaucracy, where good things can get done by an outsider who is in time and in tune with the music flowing from that old, beautiful instrument: the voice of the people. Unfortunately, where I come from, that instrument is an accordion.

Being independent is what Texas is all about. Here, I figured, someone running from the outside may have more of a chance than elsewhere of being taken seriously. In Minnesota, few people took Jesse Ventura seriously until he put them in a reverse figure-four leg lock. His confrontational style did not suit him well, however, and he lasted only one term. He didn't realize that wrestling is real and politics is fixed.

Arnold Schwarzenegger is another story. Even far into his campaign he was written off by a good part of the electorate. Then something happened to change all that: the people of California sensed that the world was watching. (They were right. We were watching Scott Peterson.) Now they all love Arnold. Many Texans are taking note, thinking that if they can get rid of politicians in California, maybe we can get rid of Californians in Texas.

So how does an independent candidate get taken seriously, particularly one who believes that humor is one of the best ways of getting to the truth? And the truth is, if we don't watch out, Guam and Samoa are going to pass us in funding of public education. Beyond its obsession with shaking down lobbyists, the Texas Legislature has proven that it is neither a visionary nor an efficient institution. The Fraternal Order of the Bulimic Moose could probably do a better, more honest, job. A good spay-and-neuter program may be the answer. As my father always said, "Treat children like adults and adults like children." But for God's sake, whether you have to go around the politicians or over them, let's get something done, even if it means invading Oklahoma so we can move up to number 48 in affordability of health care.

Here is where the spiritual lifting comes in. Though the governor of Texas is a largely ceremonial position, like the judge of a big chili cook-off, he must be able to inspire people, especially young people, to become more involved in the welfare of our state. As I drive around in my Yom Kippur Clipper (that's a Jewish Cadillac—it stops on a dime and it picks it up) I'm constantly impressed by the young people I run into, sometimes literally.

Take the young fellow I met during the campaign. He was a grocery clerk in Del Rio, and he seemed quite bright. As I was talking to him, a customer walked up and asked for half a head of lettuce. The clerk said he'd have to check with the manager, and he walked to the back of the store. Unnoticed by the clerk, the customer walked back there too, just in time to hear him say to the manager, "Some asshole wants to buy half a head of lettuce." The clerk, suddenly seeing the customer standing next to him, then turned and said, "But this kind gentleman has offered to buy the other half." Later, the manager, complimenting the clerk on his fast thinking, told him that a large Canadian chain was buying the store and suggested he might climb the ladder quickly. "Everyone in Canada," responded the clerk, "is either a hooker or a hockey player."

"Just a minute, young man," said the manager. "My wife is from Canada."

"No kiddin'," said the clerk. "Who's she play for?"

Young people like this, I believe, can serve as an inspiration to us all. Had I been elected governor, many young people would've been running the place and no doubt I'd be running after many of them. Everyone knows we're not going to get any action or inspiration from career politicians. They're so busy holding on to power they never take the time to send the elevator back down.

At the very least, I had hoped to be a candidate people can vote for, rather than against. Speaking of which, I was showing a friend around Austin recently, and he was very impressed with what he saw.

"That's a beautiful statue of Rick Perry you all put up," he said.

"That *is* Rick Perry," I said.

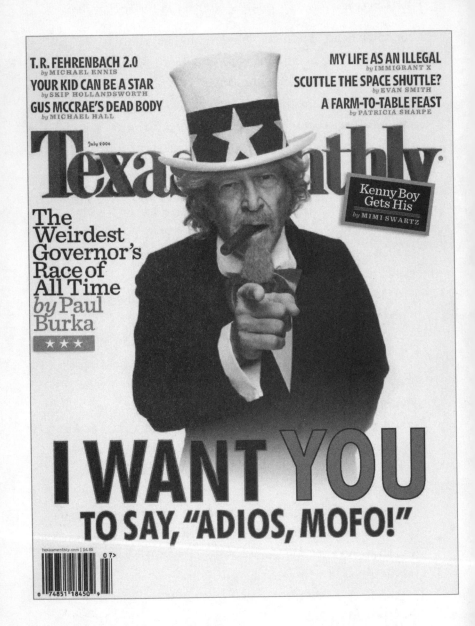

Should've been the middle finger.
(Reprinted with permission from Texas Monthly*)*

1

REMEMBER THE ALAMO AND KEEP IT HOLY

THE ALAMO
OF THE HEART

I'm not a politician, folks. Hell, I haven't even been indicted yet. I'm sixty-two years old. That's too young for
Medicare and too old for women to care. But I care
about Texas. That's why, on that wintry morning of February 3, 2005, I stood in front of the Alamo and called

for the unconditional surrender of Governor Rick Perry.

The Alamo, as most Texas schoolchildren already know, and most out-of-state tourists soon discover, is not a large or imposing structure. In fact, it is one of the smaller missions in a state where everything is supposed to be bigger. The only thing in our great state that is smaller than the Alamo, it would seem, is the voter turnout. It's been puny for many years now and these days it appears to be pretty much on life-support. Is there anything that one person like you or I can do about this pathetic situation? I believe there is and that is why I've written this book.

Because now, as politics as usual rolls across America like a noxious vapor, I'm no longer sure it matters whether the Democrats or the Republicans run the country. It's just a different swarm of locusts moving into Washington. In the words of Reverend Goat Carson, "The Republicans and the Democrats have become the same guy admiring himself in the mirror."

Texas politics really stink. The parties, whom I call the Crips and the Bloods, sell themselves to the biggest donors. Lobbyists control the legislature's agenda. Top funding groups in the state are being indicted for money-laundering. Corruption and big money have such a bipolar chokehold that the two major parties blew more than $100 million in the previous governor's race just to drive 71 percent of the voters away from the polls. After all that money was spent, less than 30 percent of us bothered to show up to vote.

Why? Because it's hard to stand in line at the ballot

box when neither candidate promises anything more than politics as usual. Texans, supposedly, are the most independent-thinking people in America, but if we're going to be inspired, the inspiration will have to come from leaders unafraid to deal in new ideas and honest answers. We need leaders who let the people call the plays instead of dancing to the tune of the moneymen. This kind of leader is never going to look or sound like a politician. He won't speak in hollow phrases, steer by image polls, or show up in hand-tailored suits.

True Texas leaders are unmistakable. After all, the last independent governor of Texas was Sam Houston. That was more than 154 years ago. He turned out to be the most visionary governor Texas has ever had. I don't believe Sam Houston would regard too highly the political landscape we see today. He would've detested the fact that we have a government of the money, by the money, and for the money. Sam never liked politicians much anyway, and neither do I. My own definition of politics goes as follows. *poly* means more than one; and *ticks* are blood-sucking parasites.

What the Alamo stood for—and fell for—mattered greatly to Sam Houston, and these ideals of courage, freedom, and independence should be precious to all of us today as well. The Daughters of the Republic of Texas have done a fine job over the years of preserving the Alamo itself as a shrine embodying all that is truly great about Texas. But what of the spiritual ramifications of the Alamo? What about the Alamo of the heart? Will Texans continue to stand in line to see Willie Nelson or Lyle

Lovett or Joe Ely, but not stand in line to vote? Have we forgotten that heroes died here to give us this right?

When I announced my candidacy for governor in front of the Alamo, the *Los Angeles Times* suggested that it might be a bad omen. They reasoned, perhaps quite logically, that the site of Texas's most famous defeat was very probably not the most fortuitous venue for the man who would be governor to begin his great quest. I believe the Alamo was the perfect place to start. It was, indeed, the only place. For when Colonel Travis took his sword and drew that spiritually indelible line in the sand, when the men of the Alamo crossed it knowing full well they were going to die, it was, more than any other, the moment that Texas was born.

A BAND OF GYPSIES
ON A PIRATE SHIP

My race for governor was never a political campaign; it was always a spiritual quest. It was populated by a group of people from outside politics who were basically searching for the soul of Texas. Often during the heat of the campaign, Willie Nelson's words brought great comfort and direction to me: "Fortunately, we're not in control."

Suits, lobbyists, fat cats, and lawyers were few and far between on our team. With just a few notable exceptions, which I'll get to presently, the vast majority of our staff had never been anywhere near a political campaign. Indeed, it sometimes seemed that everybody in our organization was either a hairstylist or a bass player. They came from all over Texas, Maine, California, England, Germany, and everywhere else reachable by the Internet and word of mouth. Even my old friend, Piers Akerman, super-journalist from Australia, came to Texas to lend his considerable weight to the campaign effort. They all came to the fair to see the bear. By the end of the experience we probably had the youngest, smartest, best-educated, most idealistic, most overworked, most underpaid, and most heartbreakingly innocent campaign staff ever assembled for a statewide race.

On the morning of February 3, 2005, however, the vast majority of these people were merely a twinkle in the candidate's eye. As dawn broke over the Alamo, a hardy group of several hundred Texans braved the frigid temperatures to fill the courtyard behind me as I did my first national interview with my friend Don Imus. Imus told me after the election that he believed racism was the cause of Harold Ford's defeat in Tennessee and apathy was the cause of mine in Texas. I told Imus we didn't really lose; we just got outscored.

But on that morning, before Imus's vast radio and television audience, hope was in the air. Emily Dickinson's "thing with feathers" was perching in the soul of Texas. All the usual suspects were there, of course. I looked around me and saw Little Jewford ("He's a Jew and he drives a Ford"), a former member of my band, the Texas Jewboys, who, among many other talents, plays the most irritating instrument in the musical kingdom, the kazoo. Also Steve "Beano" Boynton, a larger-than-life cowboy who can, and often does, fart on command; the Reverend Goat Carson, in full Indian regalia, who once wrote, "Between the gutter and the stars/People are what people are"; Cleve Hattersley, who set up the Alamo event and road-managed one of my musical tours of Australia designated as the "Take Me Home in Your Pouch Tour"; and Jason "Chicken Dick" Hardison, a savvy twenty-three-year-old who managed to insinuate himself into almost every photograph taken of me throughout the campaign. These people knew virtually nothing about politics yet they, like many others, would play seminal roles in the days to come.

Before I knew it, Imus was firing questions at me and I was doing my best to answer. One-liners from Kent Perkins, my personal Karl Rove, were helpful in the early going. Kent is a private investigator who's not only an old friend of mine, but who also happens to be married to star of stage, screen, and television Ruth Buzzi. Imus's first questions went something like this:

> *Imus:* So, how many supporters do you think you have, Kinky?
>
> *Kinky:* I don't know how many supporters I have but they all carry guns.
>
> *Imus:* Are you worried about not having as much money for the campaign as Rick Perry?
>
> *Kinky:* A fool and his money are soon elected.
>
> *Imus:* Why are you running for governor, Kinky?

> *Kinky:* I'm running for governor because I need the closet space.

These kinds of one-liners were gobbled up by the media at first but would eventually wear thin as you will soon see. Personally, I see nothing wrong with a good one-liner if it strikes the right truthful chord. I pointed out to the media that I was not the only king of one-liners. There were Mark Twain, Oscar Wilde, Henny Youngman, and Jesus Christ, in, of course, a random and haphazard order. And then there was Colonel Travis, who, one night long ago had drawn, in that little mission behind me, the cradle of Texas independence, that brave, bloody, beautiful one line in the sand, a line more impervious than our border with Mexico, a line the ends of which seem to go on forever, as they reach inexorably deeper into the sands of time. Anyway, Santa Anna's bloodthirsty hordes of Mexicans were now gone, replaced by the hordes of bloodthirsty media. As Willie Nelson always says, "Fuck 'em if they can't take a joke."

I told Imus during the interview that we were a band of Gypsies on a pirate ship and we were settin' sail for the Governor's Mansion. This, indeed, was a fairly apt description of the ragtag army now populating the courtyard of the Alamo. The band of Gypsies on a pirate ship (given to me by Dave Casstevens of the *Fort Worth Star-Telegram* and given to him by the bearded lady of one of the last freak shows in America) represented everything that was right with the campaign and everything that was wrong with it. Absolutely no one with us seemed to have any political experience or expertise. Therein, perhaps, lay our charm. And, as our soon-to-be campaign director, Senator Dean Barkley from Minnesota, never failed to remind me: "Be charming. Don't be like them."

BLESSED IS THE MATCH THAT KINDLES THE FLAME

Two spiritual bookends also weighed in on the Imus interview, blessing the campaign and blessing Texas to a congregation that included the media of the world. The New Testament was represented by my personal spiritual advisor, Billy Joe Shaver. The Old Testament was represented by my old childhood chum, Rabbi James Lee "Kiss-Tits" Kessler of Galveston. I did not introduce him in that particular fashion, however. Possibly with political decorum in mind, Imus, as well, refrained from referring to me in his usual manner, as Richard Kinky "Big Dick" Friedman. That was fine with me. In the immortal words of Willie Nelson, "I have outlived my dick."

Rabbi Jimmy and Billy Joe continued to be significant spiritual forces throughout the long days and nights ahead. They helped inspire me to do my job as I saw it—inspiring the people of Texas. The hundreds of shivering souls in front of the Alamo shouted words of encouragement, with this scene to be repeated throughout the campaign all across this great state until Billy Joe was fi-

"If you're old enough to fight in Iraq, you're old enough to help us fix Texas." —San Angelo Summer Fest
(Photo by Little Jewford)

nally sidelined by a leg-wrestling accident in Las Vegas.

I'm not sure about the Jews present (I doubt if there was a *minyan* at the Alamo), but the gentiles loved it when Rabbi Jimmy launched into his Hebrew translations of biblical blessings. They appeared blissful and just a bit confused, as if they weren't quite sure if they were being saved or being cursed with seven years of bad sex.

Billy Joe Shaver, as well as being a Texas country music icon, provided great comfort and encouragement to me personally. He also bestowed an already slogan-heavy campaign with two of its most crucial and constant credos, "If you don't love Jesus, go to hell," and "May the God of your choice bless you." We thought so highly of these two transcendental truths that we included both of them in the vocabulary of the forthcoming Kinky Friedman Talking Action Figure, a vocabulary almost as large as that of many of the people who purchased the TAF, as it was later called. (The candidate was often seen to bristle when the TAF was called a "doll." By the later months of the campaign I was relating to the TAF better than to most people and came to regard it as a close personal friend. That's when I realized I was in danger of becoming a politician myself.)

The issues, ideas, and dreams I cherished and propounded during the tortuous course of the campaign are still there like the stars at night, deep in the heart of Texas. They are still in my own heart as well. And that precious little shrine, the Alamo, is still there too, warming her handsome battle-scarred visage in the sun, braving the rain and the cold and the tourists.

If you stand in front of the Alamo for a while, you can actually hear the tourists commenting. One refrain I've often heard from out-of-staters goes something like this (supply your own Wisconsin or Long Island accent): "I can't believe it's so small. I expected it to be bigger." Sure you did. The Alamo can't match in mere size the skyscrapers of Dallas or the Astrodome in Houston. But this small mission represents the living spirit of what Texas has most to be proud of—fierce, courageous, hell-bent, never-say-die independence.

Translated to politics, we would call this spirit "the middle-finger vote." These protest voters, no matter how many or how few, should never be taken lightly, for they represent the very spark that ignited the Texas Revolution, not to mention the American Revolution. So, while the Alamo was indubitably Texas's most famous defeat, the effortlessly eternal choice made by the men of the Alamo, and the brave, bloody, beautiful way they fell, inspired many people and led directly to Sam Houston's glorious victory at the Battle of San Jacinto, which was the impetus for the creation of the state of Texas.

Blessed is the match that kindles the flame.

Scene through a window by award-winning photo-journalist Erin Trieb.
(Photo by Erin Trieb)

2

THOU SHALT NOT COVET THY NEIGHBOR'S MUDFLAPS

OR

The Long-Term Effects of Apathy upon the Yellow Rose of Texas

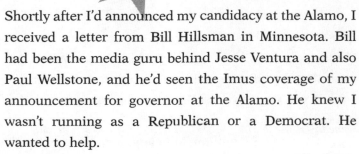

Shortly after I'd announced my candidacy at the Alamo, I received a letter from Bill Hillsman in Minnesota. Bill had been the media guru behind Jesse Ventura and also Paul Wellstone, and he'd seen the Imus coverage of my announcement for governor at the Alamo. He knew I wasn't running as a Republican or a Democrat. He wanted to help.

After several conversations with Bill, I became

aware of who my real enemy was. It was not the incumbent governor, Rick Perry. It was apathy. According to
Hillsman, the longtime stranglehold of the two-party
system had had a great deal to do with creating that
voter apathy, the sense of why bother because nothing
was going to change anyway. Texas, said Bill, was not
like Minnesota. The turnout in 1998 when Jesse Ventura
became governor of Minnesota was 62 percent; the
turnout in the most recent Texas governor's race had
been 29 percent. The fact that the traditional Texas
turnout was so pathetically low, Bill said, was bad
enough; what made it worse was that the Republicans
and Democrats liked it that way. That was how they
hung on to power.

Apathy, if allowed to go unchecked long enough,
will destroy anything: a great love affair, a great talent, a
great state. Hillsman believed that often the politicians,
pollsters, and pundits were all complicit in suppressing
the vote. So how could I awaken that slumbering giant of
Texas independence? Could one Jewish cowboy who
speaks the truth ever succeed in beating the system? And
what was all this going to cost?

These were some of the questions I'd saved for Bill
Hillsman when I met up with him about a month later in
Minneapolis on a book tour. He told me a great and sad
truth that day. If you want to succeed in politics at any
level, if you want to defeat apathy, the weapon of choice
is money.

"Give me $2 million for campaign ads on televi-
sion," said Hillsman, "and the election will be in God's

hands. Give me $5 million, and I'll take it out of God's hands and you'll be the governor of Texas."

I thought we'd be able to give Bill the $5 million, but over the course of an almost two-year campaign, including the huge hurdle of getting on the ballot as an independent, we could not come up with the cash. We did raise over $5 million—but by "nut-cuttin' time," the last forty-five days—we were only able to spend $1 million for the all-important television ad campaign. "Not even enough," as I told Hillsman later, "to put the election into God's hands."

"It is a government of the money, by the money, and for the money," John Jay Hooker, the distinguished former mayor of Nashville, told me. I didn't really believe him at the time. Jerry Springer also offered me an interesting insight during a radio interview. "Don't you understand, Kinky," he said, "that you can't tell the truth and succeed in politics." I didn't really want to believe that either.

Back in Minnesota, Hillsman was introducing me to a big guy who he said might be a possible campaign director for my fledgling foray into politics. "The real brains behind Jesse Ventura's victory," said Hillsman. The man was Senator Dean Barkley, whom Jesse had appointed to the United States Senate when Paul Wellstone had died in a plane crash. Dean had been Jesse's campaign director.

Hillsman left Dean and me alone together. We made some small talk, had a few drinks, and then came to what I like to refer to as that *Chariots of Fire* moment. Dean looked me in the eyes and said, "Why do you want to be governor?" I looked Dean square in the eye and said, "Because I love Texas and I don't like what's happening to her and I'd like to see if I can help turn things around." Dean nodded several times as if he was satisfied with my answer. "You know," said Dean, "it was important how you answered that question. I won't sign on with just anybody. In fact, I turned down Donald Trump when he asked me to run his campaign for president. So you see, I do have some principles."

I liked Dean and Bill and pretty soon we were on our way to slay the dragon of voter apathy and change politics as usual in Texas forever. The Minnesota Mafia, as I often referred to them, most likely knew how difficult it would be to run without the blessing of the two-party system. I, of course, knew virtually nothing about politics. In fact, I considered this ignorance to be one of my long suits. My other long suit was my preachin' coat, which I vowed to wear on my victorious march into the Governor's Mansion. In a better world, that might have happened. In a better world, no doubt, we might have had a better political system. We might have taken the advice of George Washington, who wanted nothing to do with political parties. All politics needed, he said, was "common sense and common honesty."

In the governor's race of 2006, only a pathetic 28 percent of eligible voters bothered to cast their ballots. In the previous governor's race, only 29 percent voted. Yet, according to Paul Burka, chief political writer at *Texas Monthly* magazine, "If every registered voter in the state

With Jesse Ventura in Luling. "He just didn't realize that wrestling is real and politics is fixed."
(Photo by Little Jewford)

were required by law to cast a ballot, Rick Perry would be out of a job and Kinky Friedman would be governor."

Perhaps that's why I sometimes feel like a knight in rusty armor that God or a small child left out in the rain, still preparing to polish that fated foil for one more round with Don Quixote's windmill, still feeling in my weather-beaten soul that timeless, visceral yearning to joust with the ever-so-slowly turning.

The situation is so sorry that it manages to be pathetic and apathetic at the same time. As long as Texans have their big hairy steaks at the Golden Corral and their four-wheeled-penis pickup trucks, the only things really missing from their lives will be their neighbor's mudflaps. People are so disgusted with the politicians that they've turned off on politics, which is exactly what the politicians wanted to happen. No matter what the Crips and the Bloods may try to tell you, their ultimate goal is to suppress the vote. They both have their pollsters and their voter rolls and they both know that if a historically large turnout were to occur, they would no longer control the process.

And we, the people, through massive, endemic apathy, have become their enablers. To paraphrase Mark Twain, we don't vote because we believe that would only encourage them.

So did our fledgling independent campaign really make any difference at all? Whenever I ask myself that question, I think of the time that Henry Kissinger was interviewing Chairman Mao. During the course of their wide-ranging talks, Kissinger asked him if he thought the

French Revolution had made any difference. "Too soon to tell," answered Chairman Mao.

I do know that one night in Austin, as I was being driven across a field in a golf cart during the South by Southwest festival, a young man held up a beer can in a salute as I passed by. "The *real* governor!" he said.

3

NEVER SAY FUCK IN FRONT OF A C-H-I-L-D

NO TEACHER LEFT BEHIND

As the Reverend Goat Carson says, "It takes a real dumbass not to understand the value of an education." It's become pretty clear to me that "No child left behind" has failed miserably. It's merely managed to leave all the children behind. That's why I say, "No teacher left behind." They are the ones the system depends upon and they are the ones getting screwed, blued, and tattooed by the state. The teachers have 100 percent accountability while the parents and the kids have zero. This glaring inequity has got to be brought into balance. Because of political correctness, shamefully low pay, politics as usual, and general neglect on the part of the powers that be, good teachers are bailing out of education into less rewarding but more profitable fields of endeavor. The only way we're ever going to get education back on track in Texas, I'm convinced, is to leave one governor behind. We had our chance and we didn't do it. Now it's four more years of suffer little children.

During the campaign I often yapped about Texas being fiftieth in education. We are last in high school kids getting to college. We are first in dropouts. Our teachers are paid well below the national average, this in a state that may well be the richest in the whole country. The *Dallas Morning News,* however, took issue with me, contending that Kinky was wrong. We're only forty-sixth in education. I rest my case. We're at, or very near, the bottom. By the way, when the *Dallas Morning News* asked me where I'd gotten my information that we were fiftieth in education, I told them I'd heard it from a peasant with a withered arm.

I don't blame Rick Perry for the mess education is in. He's only symptomatic of the situation. He's only one player and most of the time he's on the bench. As Lyndon Johnson once observed, "Education is not a problem; education is an opportunity." We have always had the opportunity to provide a better education for our kids and to pay our teachers better, but this requires real leadership, not just political leadership. Education is one of the

PEACE CORPS. This is an idea that's
 heart because I served in the Peace
 back in the 1960s. The idea was given to
en's mom, Nancy. The plan is to mobilize
 have the most wisdom and love to give),
elebrities, and members of the community to
 the public schools teaching art, shop, music,
kills, and everything else that isn't on the TAKS
Texas Peace Corps program won't cost the state
nd it'll reinvigorate the community into the pub-
ool system as well as providing our kids a truly
ounded education.

ncy Green is an investment banker and predicts that she
ould walk into any fourth-grade class and in half an hour
teach those kids how to balance a checkbook and they
would never forget for the rest of their lives. This is a skill,
I must confess, that even I don't possess. Jerry Jeff Walker
claims that if he were going to school today he would
never have become a singer-songwriter or written such hits
as "Mr. Bojangles." The TAKS test, low pay, political correctness, and sheer neglect on the parts of our elected officials have taken the joy, the heart, and the effectiveness out
of education in Texas. I don't have all the answers, but education, I'm convinced, must become the centerpiece on
he table of Texas. Any society ignores it at their peril.

areas in which you can clearly see the difference between
a politician and a statesman. A politician is merely thinking about the next election; a statesman is thinking about
the next generation. The Texas Legislature, unfortunately,
is hardly thinking at all.

The first thing that needs to be done is to appoint
people to the education system who've actually seen the
inside of a classroom. It's really very simple—put the
teachers back in charge. Teaching is the noblest profession of them all. It's not the oldest, of course. The oldest,
folks, is politics.

After a campaign stump speech in Terlingua, a
schoolteacher hugged me and I noticed that she had tears
in her eyes. I thought the lady was drunk or something
until that scenario repeated itself in other places many
times. I soon realized that, if you really care about education in Texas, you probably should have tears in your eyes.

Here are some of the suggestions I believe will help
to improve the education system:

* INCREASE TEACHER SALARIES. We are currently
$6,000 below the national average.
* THE TRUST FOR TEXAS HEROES. This is an idea my
friend Danny Davis, a Houston-based oilman, came up
with, and Dean Barkley provided the finishing touches. It
involves a one percent surcharge on big oil and big gas at
the wellhead. (This will not cause prices at the pump to
go up in Texas—most big oil and big gas produced in
Texas goes to the Yankees up north.) And here's the good
part: the billions raised by the Trust for Texas Heroes

goes directly and exclusively toward raising the salaries of teachers, cops, and firefighters. This is visionary legislation and someday it will be enacted. At the moment, however, how can you look at the Texas Legislature and still believe in intelligent design?

• TRANSFER SPORTS FUNDING out of the education budget and let the corporate sector bid on high school football stadiums, athletic directors, and soon. This will not only slash the education budget—it'll improve the sports programs as well.

• GET RID OF "TEACHING TO THE TEST." The TAKS test—Texas Assessment of Knowledge & Skills—shouldn't be the sole focus of education in Texas. No good teacher wants to teach to the test, no great teacher ever will. That's a major reason why we're losing our best educators. I have yet to find a kid or a parent who thinks the TAKS test is a good idea, either. It has created a whole generation of supposedly college-bound kids who aren't quite sure if the Civil War took place here or in Europe. It wasn't on the test. They've never heard of Mark Twain. He wasn't on the test. The TAKS test, as well, has the added bad feature of severely penalizing special ed students, making it almost impossible for them to be effectively mainstreamed. Teachers now fear to have them in their classes as they may draw down the precious TAKS test numbers, thereby affecting their jobs and their salaries. The narrow, artificial constraints of teaching to the test have created a meaningless, highly ineffective method of educating children. It's the primary reason we're dead last in high school kids making it to college.

With Texas Monthly *editor Evan Smith on-troducing him to my date.*
(Photo by Brian Kanof)

areas in which you can clearly see the difference between a politician and a statesman. A politician is merely thinking about the next election; a statesman is thinking about the next generation. The Texas Legislature, unfortunately, is hardly thinking at all.

The first thing that needs to be done is to appoint people to the education system who've actually seen the inside of a classroom. It's really very simple—put the teachers back in charge. Teaching is the noblest profession of them all. It's not the oldest, of course. The oldest, folks, is politics.

After a campaign stump speech in Terlingua, a schoolteacher hugged me and I noticed that she had tears in her eyes. I thought the lady was drunk or something until that scenario repeated itself in other places many times. I soon realized that, if you really care about education in Texas, you probably should have tears in your eyes.

Here are some of the suggestions I believe will help to improve the education system:

• INCREASE TEACHER SALARIES. We are currently $6,000 below the national average.

• THE TRUST FOR TEXAS HEROES. This is an idea my friend Danny Davis, a Houston-based oilman, came up with, and Dean Barkley provided the finishing touches. It involves a one percent surcharge on big oil and big gas at the wellhead. (This will not cause prices at the pump to go up in Texas—most big oil and big gas produced in Texas goes to the Yankees up north.) And here's the good part: the billions raised by the Trust for Texas Heroes

41

goes directly and exclusively toward raising the salaries of teachers, cops, and firefighters. This is visionary legislation and someday it will be enacted. At the moment, however, how can you look at the Texas Legislature and still believe in intelligent design?

- TRANSFER SPORTS FUNDING out of the education budget and let the corporate sector bid on high school football stadiums, athletic directors, and soon. This will not only slash the education budget—it'll improve the sports programs as well.

- GET RID OF "TEACHING TO THE TEST." The TAKS test—Texas Assessment of Knowledge & Skills—shouldn't be the sole focus of education in Texas. No good teacher wants to teach to the test, no great teacher ever will. That's a major reason why we're losing our best educators. I have yet to find a kid or a parent who thinks the TAKS test is a good idea, either. It has created a whole generation of supposedly college-bound kids who aren't quite sure if the Civil War took place here or in Europe. It wasn't on the test. They've never heard of Mark Twain. He wasn't on the test. The TAKS test, as well, has the added bad feature of severely penalizing special ed students, making it almost impossible for them to be effectively mainstreamed. Teachers now fear to have them in their classes as they may draw down the precious TAKS test numbers, thereby affecting their jobs and their salaries. The narrow, artificial constraints of teaching to the test have created a meaningless, highly ineffective method of educating children. It's the primary reason we're dead last in high school kids making it to college.

With Texas Monthly *editor Evan Smith on his TV show. Here I'm introducing him to my date.*
(Photo by Brian Kanof)

• THE TEXAS PEACE CORPS. This is an idea that's very close to my heart because I served in the Peace Corps in Borneo back in the 1960s. The idea was given to me by Pat Green's mom, Nancy. The plan is to mobilize retirees (who have the most wisdom and love to give), musicians, celebrities, and members of the community to volunteer in the public schools teaching art, shop, music, vocation skills, and everything else that isn't on the TAKS test. The Texas Peace Corps program won't cost the state a dime and it'll reinvigorate the community into the public school system as well as providing our kids a truly well-rounded education.

Nancy Green is an investment banker and predicts that she could walk into any fourth-grade class and in half an hour teach those kids how to balance a checkbook and they would never forget for the rest of their lives. This is a skill, I must confess, that even I don't possess. Jerry Jeff Walker claims that if he were going to school today he would never have become a singer-songwriter or written such hits as "Mr. Bojangles." The TAKS test, low pay, political correctness, and sheer neglect on the parts of our elected officials have taken the joy, the heart, and the effectiveness out of education in Texas. I don't have all the answers, but education, I'm convinced, must become the centerpiece on the table of Texas. Any society ignores it at their peril.

HOW DO WE PAY FOR ALL OF THIS?

This one's a no-brainer—legalize casino gambling in Texas. We invented Texas Hold 'Em and we can't even play it here! Billions and billions of dollars are pouring out of Texas on a regular basis, fueling the economies of Louisiana, Oklahoma, New Mexico, Mississippi, and, my personal favorite, Las Vegas. Even the Indian casinos in Texas have been shut down by this narrow, misguided, hypocritical policy. We have people in East Texas who go to church Sunday morning and go to Shreveport Sunday night. Now the Louisiana gambling establishment is mad at Oklahoma for taking their Texans away. I say, legalize casino gambling and do it now. Bring the money back to Texas and pay for education once and for all. We're first in dropouts and thirty-second in education spending and, to paraphrase Frank Sinatra, we're losing. I just recently returned from a little fact-finding trip to Las Vegas, and I can assure you, virtually everybody there seems to be from Texas. Texas has the most money and the most people but we're being played for suckers because our politicians lack common sense.

With the billions of dollars we could easily realize by legalizing casino gambling, not to mention "slots for tots"—slot machines at racetracks and convenience stores—we could take, at the very least, two giant steps forward in education. We could pay our teachers what they deserve, and we could send every high school kid with a B average or better to college free.

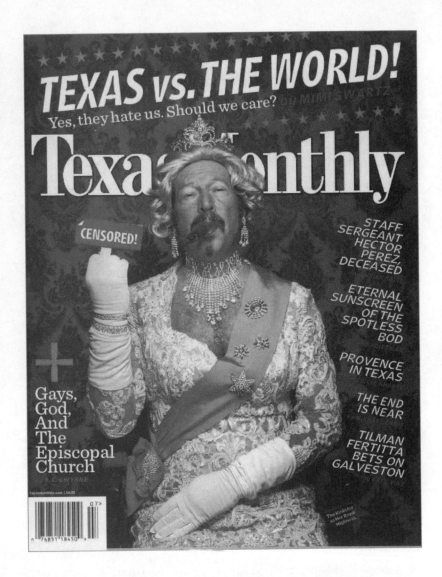

Some people will do anything to get a date with Rick Perry
(Reprinted with permission from Texas Monthly)

4

THOU
SHALT
FIGHT
WUSSIFICATION

 W W W R D

Early on in the campaign I came out strongly against wussification, which is the weakening of fibers, be they physical, moral, or spiritual. I vowed to beat wussification if I had to do it one wuss at a time. Many mocked my anti-wussification efforts and believed it all had to be a joke. I usually responded by asking, "WWWRD?" What

Would Will Rogers Do? I followed up by quoting Will Rogers, who claimed to feel very much at home with the politicians. "The politicians are the greatest comedians of them all," he said. "The only trouble is, every time they make a joke it turns into a law, and every time they make a law, it turns into a joke."

The anti-wussification campaign, I assured them, was no joke. The joke, I said, was the Texas Legislature. I railed against the PC police that had practically turned tobacco users into biblical lepers. I talked about the way many people were ashamed to say "Merry Christmas" these days. I pointed out that I was a Je-e-e-w-w-w and I didn't mind a bit. I said that I hated the way the Ten Commandments had been taken out of the public schools. I wanted to bring them back. "We might have to rename them," I said. "We might have to call them 'The Ten Suggestions.' "

After all, I reasoned, it was most likely the objections of just one atheist that got them removed in the first place. One atheist doesn't like something and out it goes. And we all know what happens to an atheist when he dies. His tombstone usually reads: All dressed up and no place to go.

Texas, I've always believed, is the last line of defense against creeping political correctness in America. If we lose the battle here, we've all lost for good. And most people don't know the name of the man who coined the phrase "political correctness." I'll tell you. It was Joseph Stalin. So it seems highly ironic to me that liberals are the ones who appear to champion it today. I'm against those left-wing liberals who are embarrassed to say Merry Christmas. I'm also against those far-right religious folks who are largely responsible for keeping legalized gambling out of Texas. These two relatively small fringe groups are, in my opinion, holding back the greatest state in the country.

During the long, sometimes tedious course of the gubernatorial campaign, there were many instances of the PC police attempting to crimp the style of the Kinkster. Because of an oral fixation, and because it's my magic feather, I virtually always have a Cuban cigar in my mouth. I smoke about eight to ten Cuban cigars a day. I'm quick to point out, however, that I'm not supportin' their economy; I'm burnin' their fields.

Nevertheless, whenever I appeared on television actually smoking a cigar, no one ever heard what my comments were because legions of officious e-mailers pelted the station in their astonishment that a man with a cowboy hat was smoking a cigar. There were worse things going on in the state, like the complete neglect of immigration, education, and the environment, but you wouldn't have known it. I held on to the cigar for dear life but eventually it was the better part of valor to stop smoking it in public. This of course caused people to constantly come up to me and ask, "Do you ever smoke that thing?" or "Is that thing lit?" To the latter question I would often respond, "Which thing are you referring to?" which was, of course, a veiled reference to my penis. This response, I suspect, may have cost me some votes in the suburbs.

This obsession with political correctness is just not common sense. If three men were to walk into a Dallas restaurant, one with an Uzi submachine gun, one stark naked, and one wearing a cowboy hat and smoking a cigar, who do you think would get the attention of the maître d' first? The customers would run hither and thither, they'd arrest the guy with the cigar, and the naked man and the guy with the machine gun would be left there wondering where the hell everybody went. All this focus on minutiae in a state that's number one in executions, toll roads, and property taxes, and ranked last in health care coverage, education, and care for the elderly.

Woody Guthrie once said, "The more laws you make, the more criminals you're going to have." That's why there are more people in the Texas prison system than the entire population of Alaska. It's also what's been killing Austin's world-famous live music scene.

The smoking regulations in Austin are what I consider to be one of the most shameful examples of wussification. The so-called civic leaders will tell you that the new anti-smoking regulations have not resulted in lessened revenues for food or beverages in Austin. What they don't tell you is that the vast majority of food and beverage sales are now being generated by Bennigan's, Chili's, Applebee's, and other large chains. Many of the smaller mom-and-pop historic live music venues have been wiped out by the new ordinances. Only the famous ones like the Continental Club or Antone's have managed to survive.

GUINNESSGATE, 2006

While the subject matter deals with beverages, I'd be re-miss if I did not mention Guinness, the drink that kept the Irish from taking over the world, and almost kept me from getting on the ballot. That's because the media are always ready to side with the dark forces of wussification. And wussification, to paraphrase Ernest Hemingway, is political correctness's little sister. Personally, I believe po-litical correctness is this country's biggest threat when it comes to independent thinking and freedom of speech. You would think the media would eschew political cor-rectness, but the opposite is, unfortunately, true; for the most part, they embrace it. The media are essentially lazy and it's much easier to resort to "Got ya!" journalism than it is to speak up for the truth.

A classic example of this came in April 2006 just as our petition drive to get my name on the ballot as an in-dependent was going into high gear. I'd accepted an offer to be grand marshal of the big St. Patrick's Day parade in Dallas. Yes, that's right, folks—Kinky McFriedman. With my friend Pauley Hines driving his brightly decorated or-ange and blue Prowler and Little Jewford riding shotgun, I was perched on the back like an aging beauty queen and waving to the crowd when Senator Dean Barkley walked by and handed me a Guinness. This wasn't hard for him to do. The vehicle was stuck in the huge parade and mov-ing at a speed of about one mile per hour.

Sipping Guinness at the St. Patrick's Day Parade in Dallas. "I did not swallow."
*(Photo by David Woo/*The Dallas Morning News ©)

I was smoking a cigar and sipping the Guinness from the can and generally having a great time being grand marshal of the parade. It was probably a little bit more difficult to be grand marshal, I remember reflecting at the time, than it was to be a ribbon-cutter figurehead governor. I was totally oblivious to the fact that multiple media outlets were meticulously capturing me in the act of breaking a state law, the "open container" law, which applies, apparently, even if you're only a passenger in the vehicle.

It was later that evening, back at the Adolphus Hotel, when our press secretary, Laura Stromberg, began frantically calling Little Jewford. According to Little Jewford, Laura was highly agitato, and "sounded like she was about to start squirtin' out of both ends." There was a major shit-storm going on in the media, apparently, and it was headed our way at 100 miles per hour.

"They're saying Kinky broke the state open container law as grand marshal," Laura told Little Jewford. "They're saying he's a bad role model. I'm getting bombarded with calls. Mothers Against Drunk Driving are getting in on it. Kinky's reputation could be ruined."

"What reputation?" said Little Jewford.

This, I felt, was wussification of the worst kind. I was being crucified by the media for taking a few sips from a can of Guinness as a passenger in a parade vehicle moving at one mile per hour surrounded by throngs of drunken young people, many of whom were on floats and in vehicles as well. And, after all, it was St. Patty's Day.

The next morning, the proverbial shit hit the proverbial fan. The *Dallas Morning News* ran a photo of me in an emerald green jacket, sitting in the open car actually drinking from what was clearly a can of Guinness. God help us all! Something had to be done or the whole campaign might make a rapid detour into the toilet. The photo and the story were already being picked up by newspapers all over Texas.

I conferred with Laura Stromberg; Reid Nelson, commander of the petition drive; Dick DeGuerin, our legal committee; Wes Kirkman, Blake Rocap, Dean, Bill, Laureen Oliver, our expert petition consultant; Kent Perkins, Debora Hanson, campaign super-scheduler; John McCall, our campaign treasurer; Farouk Shami, honorary chairman; Little Jewford, Beano, Chicken Dick, and many other people with colorful and humorous names. Should I apologize? Should I prepare to go into rehab? I remembered what Willie Nelson had once told me, "Rehab's where they go to rest up before they come back at us again."

Dean Barkley's words carried a lot of weight with me at this moment of world crisis: "Never apologize for being yourself. Don't be like them." I also remembered what Bill Clinton had told me recently when he'd come to Austin on a book tour. "Stay funny," Bill had offered. "That's the way you connect with people." He had helped me in more ways than perhaps he realized at the time.

When I, at last, released my statement regarding Guinnessgate it was almost universally well received. The young people and Joe Six-Pack loved it and MADD wasn't mad anymore. Even the *Dallas Morning News* editorialized how "refreshing" it was to see someone *not* be a typical politician, and *not* apologize or talk about rehab.

My statement, brief and to the point, was essentially as follows: "I am here to admit that I *did* drink the Guinness. But I did not swallow."

GOD BLESS OSCAR WILDE

It was around the time of Guinnessgate that the TABC, the Texas Alcoholic Beverage Commission, made national news by sending undercover cops into hotel bars to arrest drunks in Dallas. This cowardly act played perfectly into my anti-wussification campaign. If you were a drunk, I reasoned, the perfect place for you to be was in a bar. With crime, corruption, and illegal immigration being what they were, I said, this was a reprehensible misuse of law enforcement. Then I launched into the story of Oscar Wilde, always reminding my audience that I'd probably be the only candidate who'd be invoking the name of Oscar Wilde during the campaign. I was not wrong.

The story has it that Oscar Wilde was fairly well walking on his knuckles in a pub in London when he too was arrested by undercover cops. The first cop approached him and said, "Oscar Wilde?" to which Oscar responded affirmatively. The undercover guy then said, "Do you know who I am?"

Oscar Wilde then turned to the bar and said, "Good God! There's a man here who doesn't know who he is!"

Tooling around downtown Alpine with my two trusty sidekicks,
Little Jewford and Doodle.
(Photo by Melinda Joy Moore)

5

THOU SHALT THROW THE MONEY CHANGERS OUT OF THE TEMPLE

OR

I Can Answer That for You, but I Can't Understand It for You

Political reform. Why is this so important? Have you ever tried to go visit your congressman and forgotten your checkbook? Have you ever wondered who actually writes the legislation that eventually becomes the law of the land? Have you by now perhaps realized that every time a bell rings, another lobbyist gets his wings?

There are good legislators, of course, who are just as frustrated as the rest of us. But, unfortunately, they are rarely in power positions. Something about the system tends to beat you down after a while and you realize that to have any voice at all, to even get reelected, you have to go along to get along. The lobbyists and the so-called leadership are necessary evils. It's not unusual for lobbyists to write the legislation themselves and hand their bought-and-paid-for legislators their marching orders. That's why some members of the Texas Legislature have taken to calling the section of the gallery where the lobbyists sit "the owner's box."

How do we get these career politicians and lobbyists out of the system? How can we effectively clean out the political stables? The Crips and the Bloods, unfortunately, like bullies on a playground, are not going to help us attain clean government. Their mind-set has become almost entirely one of hanging on to power whatever it takes. They care much more about getting themselves reelected than they do about helping the people of Texas. A political leader should be like a Wal-Mart greeter—he should first say, "How can I help you?" Instead, the career politician enters a room full of people usually asking himself, "Who's here who can help me?" Remember, it's poly-ticks.

After having become the first man to get on the ballot as an independent in 154 years, I am in a rather unique position. I've had to leap over every hurdle and jump through every hoop the system can dream of to block my progress. The two-party system does not want to share the American stage with anyone—they want it all to themselves. George Washington, Teddy Roosevelt, Davy Crockett, and Sam Houston were not only great independent thinkers and leaders, but also enemies of the Crips and Bloods of their times. In more recent years, the two-party monopoly did everything it could to destroy Ralph Nader, Pat Buchanan, and Ross Perot. The only thing the two parties seem to agree upon is that there should be no new parties, no new people, and no new ideas. Other than that, the only time they ever get off their asses is to attack each other.

Here are some suggestions for a political reform agenda in Texas:

• SAME DAY VOTER REGISTRATION (SDVR). This reform will make it possible for people to register and vote on election day. States with SDVR enjoy anywhere from 5 percent to 25 percent higher voter turnout rates. Real democracy means getting more people into the process so the true will of the people can be accurately measured and heard. SDVR has particularly been shown to increase the participation of young people in the electoral process. Jesse Ventura told me he wouldn't have won in Minnesota without SDVR and the youth vote. This is not surprising—independent candidates often tend to attract younger and newer voters. It will also, however, encourage many voters who do not become interested in the campaigns until just weeks before an election, by which time in Texas, registration rolls are closed. These people, whom Dean Barkley likes to not unkindly refer to as "cave dwellers," represent the majority of people in our state. Why would anyone want to keep young voters, new voters, and the majority of citizens of our state away from the polls? Next time you meet up with the Crips or the Bloods you might ask them what they're so afraid of.

- MANDATORY VOTING. This sounds bad but it really isn't. Australia's been doing it with great success for some time now. It works like this. Every citizen is required to show up at the polls and have his or her name checked off. If you don't show up, you're fined something like fifty bucks. You don't have to vote, but in Australia, the turnouts are often as high as 98 percent and political corruption has plummeted. If we had mandatory voting in Texas I'd be in the Governor's Mansion right now with my five dogs, the Friedmans, and we'd all be smoking Cuban cigars.

- FAIR BALLOT ACCESS. Texas is one of the two most difficult states for an independent candidate or a new party to get on the ballot. What's the other state? I don't know. The peasant with the withered arm wouldn't tell me. Maybe you can Google it when you get home. The point is that petition requirements in Texas are outdated and impractical and the powers that be like it that way. We had to collect over 45,000 signatures in a very short period of time and they all had to be notarized. We succeeded in getting almost four times that number but, believe me, it wasn't something I'd ever want to have to do again. And nobody should have to do it. Just place independent candidates on the primary ballots of each major party, allowing voters to participate in the party nomination process while also supporting an independent candidate's attempt to be placed on the general election ballot. This would not only increase voter turnout, it would also encourage participation in the democratic process. From Sam Houston to Kinky Friedman is a very long time between dreams.

• INITIATIVE AND REFERENDUM. I like to call it I&R. Texas does not currently allow citizens this right, but it should. It's the reason women's suffrage, labor rights, Social Security, and many other reforms were won in America. Most Texans, for instance, favor legalized casino gambling and do not favor toll roads. Real political reforms occur when citizens are able to place their own initiatives on the ballot.

• FAIR AND OPEN DEBATES. First of all, there were no "debates." There was one lousy debate, thanks to one man, Governor Rick Perry. That one stilted, game-show-type of event was held on Texas-OU Weekend, one of the biggest football games of the year, a time that would attract the least amount of viewers possible. Perry backed out of at least six other chances to debate that were offered. Jesse Ventura told me that in the Minnesota governor's race, he participated in more than sixteen debates, many of them televised statewide. He didn't really get the hang of it and begin kicking his opponents' asses until he had a few under his belt. That's because, when the debate is stage-managed by political handlers, it'll always result in a *Jeopardy!*-like situation favoring slick career politicians over newcomers every time. I'm not making excuses. I thought of a lot of good answers, but most of them were in the car going home. By then, of course, "the debate" was over.

The Great Debate. Don't touch that remote.
(Photo by Erin Trieb)

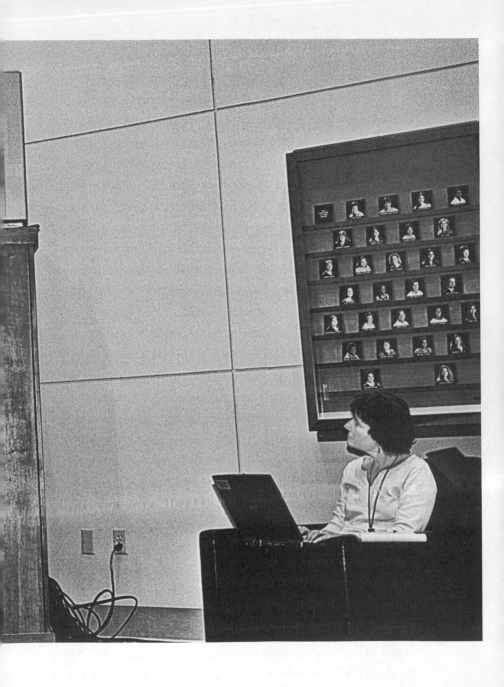

A nonpartisan entity should be established to develop fair and clear criteria for inclusion of all qualified candidates into the debates. And there should be many debates—the more, the merrier—not one sorry excuse.

- PUBLICLY FUNDED CAMPAIGNS. Special interest money is the lifeblood of most candidates. When those candidates are elected, they use political appointments and legislation that favors those special interests as payback. Privately financed campaigns have disenfranchised too many Texans for too long, and incumbents spend more time fund-raising for reelection than they do working for the citizens who elected them.

Publicly financed campaigns, funded through surcharges and registration fees on lobbyists, would eliminate the influence of special interests and would level the playing field for all political candidates. Increased registration fees for lobbyists and 10 percent surcharges on lobbying expenditures and other independent expenditures would provide more than $30 million in funding for Texas legislative and statewide races.

Texas should also join the six other states—Arizona, Maine, Massachusetts, New Mexico, North Carolina, and Vermont—that have adopted Clean Money Campaign Reform laws. The system offers full public financing for candidates who agree to spending limits and reject private contributions.

- LOBBYING REFORM. Stop the revolving door between state service and lobbying. Place a ban on any Texas elected official or Texas state employee from becoming a lobbyist in Texas for two years from the time he leaves or retires from his state position.

- REDISTRICTING REFORM. The practice of allowing elected officials to draw their own election districts must stop. This type of political extremism lets the party in power take unfair advantage, and results in less competition in our elections. We propose using the Iowa model of a nonpartisan redistricting commission. In light of the myriad political scandals that have dominated the headlines for the past year, it has become increasingly clear that we must end our anything-goes system and restore honesty and integrity to Texas politics.

As I always say, "Politics is the only field in which the more experience you have, the worse you get."

My personal advice to all Texans and all Americans in the world is very, very simple: Never reelect anybody.

"Musicians can better run this state than politicians."
(Photo by Jody Rhoden)

6

THOU SHALT NOT BULLSHIT

OR
Sacred Teachings of the Butt-Sniffing Clan

A bullshitter is a euphemism for a politician. You can't quite catch him in a lie, but then neither does the truth ever seem to escape his lips. Thus, as a truth-teller can sometimes be seen as a dealer in hope, a politician is by nature a dealer in false hope. The politician quite often can't help himself; deviousness, deception, and duplicity are the ways of his people. Right from the very beginning, as a candidate for governor, I only claimed to have three real qualifications: I could ride, shoot straight, and tell the truth.

I've always liked stray dogs better than fat cats. I believe the governor should go on radio and television talk shows and answer real questions from real people. The governor, if he truly wants to be the governor of the people, should install a listed phone number to the Governor's Mansion and take calls from the people during certain hours every day. These calls should not be monitored for quality control. This will probably never come to pass, of course, but it's a great idea.

There are many reasons why most people don't vote in Texas, and perhaps justifiably, why apathy is almost endemic. Nonetheless, the people seem to be drooling for the truth. They have been bullshitted by the politicians, pundits, and pollsters for so long that, although I didn't win this round, a great many Texans found my campaign to be "a breath of fresh air," even with the ubiquitous cigar smoke.

Most Republicans, for instance, I believe to be not so concerned with gay marriage, flag-burning, abortion, and other wedge issues as they are with hanging on to at least a small shard of the income they've worked for. Most Democrats, while opposed to prayer in school for the most part, realize that something spiritual seems to be missing in our society. During the campaign I openly pushed for prayer in school, saying, "What's wrong with a kid believing in something." I also strongly supported gay marriage, saying, "They have every right to be just as miserable as the rest of us." The fact that I supported prayer in school *and* gay marriage made me unique among virtually all candidates for high office in this country. That's because, in most cases, the party tells the politician what to think. On the other hand, anyone who supports both gay marriage and prayer in school has to be telling you what he believes to be the truth. In my opinion, that's one good reason to vote for anybody. A candidate who thinks for himself is always good, even if he's a little ahead of his time.

Another major subject that neither political party really wants to deal with is immigration. They tell you what you want to hear and then do absolutely nothing. It's like saying the government is creating new jobs when everybody knows only the private sector can create new jobs. All the government can create is jobs for government workers. In Texas, the politicians all tell you they're tough on crime. Are they really? Is that why we have yet to pass Jessica's Law and the prisons are choked to capacity with small-time drug offenders?

Texas may not be ready for a real governor who will cut through the bullshit. So instead, they'll have to settle for just another ribbon-cutter. Governor Perry is no different from other Republicans and Democrats, all of whom bitch and moan and pledge and promise action regarding illegal immigration, and then, for political reasons, don't do a damn thing. For the past six years Perry's policy on illegal immigration into Texas has been, "Bring us your gangs, your bombs, your drugs, your terrorists—welcome to Texas." I believe Perry, like President Bush, is a good man trapped in a Republican's body. The question they ask first is, "How will this play with the great and growing bloc of Hispanic voters?" It should be, "What's the right thing to do for America? What's the right thing for Texas?"

Tom DeLay made the same mistake of putting party first and doing whatever it takes to hang on to power. After being in politics for a while, he forgot that he was hired to serve the people of Texas. He began thinking that his main job was to attack Democrats. He merely got caught at it. That's all. His behavior is hardly the exception to the rule.

K. I. S. S. P.

There is a no-bullshit, commonsense approach to illegal immigration, crime, taxes, and government spending—issues that affect all of our lives—and we laid it out during the campaign. We called it K. I. S. S. P. Keep It Simple, Stupid Politicians. On September 6, 2006, we began unveiling the K. I. S. S. P. program at press conferences all across the state. Essentially, it is as follows:

• ILLEGAL IMMIGRATION. Texas can no longer wait for the feds to help us with our border situation. They haven't helped us in 153 years and they won't substantively do it now. Here are some steps Texas can immediately take to help stem the tide of illegal immigrants penetrating our border.

Increase the number of Texas National Guard troops

Talking with Texas Tech students at the statue of Will Rogers and his horse, Soapsud.
(Photo by Brian Kanof)

on the border to 10,000. (Perry has 1,500 there now, mostly for show since they have no authority to detain illegals and often no ammunition. When I told Don Imus that the Guard troops had weapons but no ammunition, he provided an interesting insight. "As long as the Mexicans don't know this," he said, "it just might work.")

Once the border is protected instead of neglected, we should print up foreign taxpayer ID cards for any foreigner who wants to seek employment, provided he can pass a criminal background check. If he passes the check, he gets the card and he's good to go. At that point, if we catch an employer hiring an illegal who doesn't have a foreign taxpayer ID card, we sock it to him. The fine is $25,000 the first time, and it goes up from there. The implementation of these three steps will go a long way toward respecting and protecting that line in the sand we call the border. But you can't just talk about it. You gotta do it.

• CRIME. In Houston, crime has shot up since the city opened its doors to Katrina evacuees. According to the chief of police, 23 percent of Houston's homicide rate this year can be traced directly to the evacuees. We are calling for $100 million from our state's huge budget surplus to be allocated immediately to Houston and Harris County. This will put 1,200 more cops on the street. Other cities will receive a similar allocation if they can demonstrate comparable spikes in crime.

• GOVERNMENT SPENDING/TAXES. Under Perry's watch, state spending and property taxes have increased at rates that far exceed population increases and inflation. Appraisals are out of control and Texans are being taxed out of their homes.

"These economic trends are not in line with a state," I said, "that's sitting on an $11 billion to $13 billion surplus." That was putting it mildly.

My fiscal policy would call for enacting legislation that will cap state spending, with increases adjusted for inflation, population increases, and unforeseen disasters. Under Perry, the state saw an 18 percent increase in state spending from 2004-2005 to 2005-2006, with the budget jumping from $117.4 billion to $138.2 billion.

To give Texans the property tax relief they deserve, I would also call for a cap on appraisals from the current 10 percent per year down to 3 percent. Texas is taking in more tax revenue than ever before, and we've got a huge budget surplus. Yet the politicians still want to spend your money and raise your taxes.

• PERRY'S BUSINESS TAX. Texas is the only state in the country with a tax on gross business income. Perry's business tax should be abolished. Taxing small and medium businesses hurts our state's economy and discourages new businesses from coming to Texas. This tax amounts to nothing more than a personal income tax in disguise.

Meeting with a lobbyist.
(Photo courtesy of David Woo, from Top Dogs with Their Pets.*)*

THOU
SHALT
NOT
KILL

MAX SOFFAR

A good politician, they say, should be like a good football coach. He should be smart enough to understand the game, yet dumb enough to think it means something. But there are times when politics can mean something important, perhaps even existential. The politics of which I write are the politics of life and death.

I'm not anti-death penalty; I'm anti-the-wrong-guy-getting-executed. I offer the story of Max Soffar as Exhibit A.

I'd never interviewed anyone on death row until the middle of January 2004, when I picked up a telephone and looked through the clear plastic divider at the haunting reflection of my own humanity in the eyes of Max Soffar. Max doesn't have a lot of time and neither do I, so I'll try to keep it brief and to the point. "I'm not a murderer," he told me. "I want people to know that I'm not a murderer. That means more to me than anything. It means more to me than freedom."

Somewhere along the line, Max's life fell between the cracks. A sixth-grade dropout whose IQ tests pegged him as borderline mentally retarded, he grew up in Houston, where he was a petty burglar, an idiot-savant car thief, and a low-level, if highly imaginative, police snitch. He spent four years, he says, "in the nut house in Austin," where he remembers the guards putting on human cockfights: they would lock two eleven-year-olds in a cell, egg them on, and bet on which one would be able to walk out. Max ran away, and it's been pretty much downhill from there.

For the past twenty-three years, since confessing to a cold-blooded triple murder at a Houston bowling alley, Max has been at his final station on the way: the Polunsky Unit, in Livingston. But he long ago recanted that confession, and many people, including a growing number of Houston-area law enforcement officers, think he didn't commit the crime. They say he told the cops what they wanted to hear after three days of interrogation without a lawyer present. At the very least, they say, Max's case is an example of everything that's wrong with the system. Another observer troubled by Max's case is Fifth Circuit Court of Appeals judge Harold R. DeMoss Jr., who wrote in 2002, after hearing Max's last appeal, "I have lain awake nights agonizing over the enigmas, contradictions, and ambiguities" in the record.

Chief among these Kafkaesque elements is the fact that Max's state-appointed attorney was the late Joe Cannon, who was infamous for sometimes sleeping through his clients' capital murder trials. Cannon managed to stay awake for Max's, but he did not bother to interview the one witness who might have cleared him. There are, incidentally, ten men on death row who were clients of Cannon's.

Then there's the evidence—or the total lack of it. Jim Schropp, a Washington, D.C., lawyer who's been handling Max's case for more than ten years on a pro bono basis, says it seemed cut-and-dried when he initially reviewed the file. "But the more we looked into it," he told me, "the facts and the confession didn't match up." Schropp discovered that there was no physical evidence linking Max to the crime. No eyewitnesses who placed him at the scene or saw him do it. Two police lineups in which Max was not fingered. Missing polygraphs. If the facts had been before them, Schropp says, no jurors would have believed that the prosecution's case had eliminated all reasonable doubt. "When you peel away the layers of the onion," he says, "you find a rotten core."

Okay, so what about the confession? My friend Steve Rambam, Max's pro bono private investigator, says that when Max was arrested on August 5, 1980, for speeding on a stolen motorcycle, it was the third or fourth time he'd been caught for various offenses. He thought he could deal his way out again as he'd done before. The bowling alley murders had been highly publicized, and Max had seen the police sketch of the perpetrator, which he thought resembled a friend and sometime running buddy. Max and the friend, Lat Bloomfield, were on the outs—they'd agreed to rob each of their parents' houses, but after they'd robbed Max's parents' house, Bloomfield reneged on robbing his own parents' house—so to get revenge and to help his own case in the process, Max volunteered that he knew something about the murders. Unfortunately, in his attempts to implicate his friend, he placed himself at the scene, and before long he became a target of the investigation himself. "The cops spoon-fed Max information, and he gave them what they wanted," Rambam says. "He was a confession machine. If he thought it would have helped him with the police, he would have confessed to kidnapping the Lindbergh baby."

The trouble was, Max's confession—actually, he made three different confessions—contained conflicting information. First he claimed to be outside the bowling alley when the murders took place and that he only heard the shots. Then he said he was inside and saw it all go down. Then he said his friend shot two people and threw him the gun, whereupon he shot the other two; it was like a scene in an old western. The written record of Max's confession states there were two gunmen, himself and his friend; the only surviving victim, the witness Joe Cannon didn't bother to interview, says there was only one. Max also told the cops that he and his friend had killed some people and buried them in a field. The cops used methane probes and search dogs and found nothing. He claimed they had robbed several convenience stores, which turned out never to have been robbed. Best of all, when the cops told him that the bowling alley had been burglarized the night before the murders, Max confessed to that crime as well. What he didn't know was that the burglars had already been arrested. "We won't be needing that confession," the homicide detective reportedly told him. After signing the murder confession, Max asked the officers, "Can I go home now?"

You may be wondering: What about the friend, Lat Bloomfield? He was arrested solely on the basis of Max's confession but was released because there was no evidence (the same "evidence" was later considered good enough to put Max on death row). Nonetheless, at Max's trial, the prosecutor told the jury that the police knew that Bloomfield was involved and that they planned to hunt him down once Max was dealt with.

But it never happened, and for the past twenty-three years, Bloomfield—who is the son of a Houston law enforcement officer—has been living free as a bird, currently in Mississippi, with the long arm of the Texas law never once reaching out to touch him. Why? Good question. "It wasn't hard to run him down and pay him a visit," Rambam says. "I found his name in the phone book."

Why would someone confess to a crime he didn't commit? A cry for help? A drug-addled death wish? Perhaps it has to do with what the poet Kenneth Patchen once wrote: "There are so many little dyings, it doesn't matter which of them is death."

As my interview with Max was ending, he placed his hand against the glass. I did likewise. He said he would like for me to be there with him at the execution if it happens. I hesitated. "You've come this far," he said. "Why go halfway?"

I promised him I would be there. It's a promise I would dearly love not to have to keep.

SAVE A HORSE, RIDE A COWBOY

Texas ranks not only number one in executions, it also is home to two of the three horse slaughter plants in America. More than 100,000 horses a year are slaughtered in these plants, the meat being shipped to France for human consumption. As far as I'm concerned, we either shut these plants down or we shut down France.

These are not old or sick horses. For the most part they are young and healthy, their only fault was being sold to the wrong person. The two Texas plants are in Kaufman and Fort Worth. Kaufman is about thirty miles southeast of Dallas. The mayor of Kaufman and the vast majority of its citizens would like for the Belgian-owned slaughter plant to get the hell out of Dodge and so would I. Killing American horses for French table food goes against the cowboy spirit of this state. The plant's motto is "From the stable to the table in four days." My motto is, "Save a horse, ride a cowboy."

This country was discovered, explored, and built on the back of a horse and, in the eyes of a wild mustang, one can still see a flash of that free and independent spirit that made it great. These wild mustangs, as well, are being slaughtered only to become an exotic entrée in a foreign restaurant. Our elected officials should do the right thing and close down this disgraceful operation. It does not belong anywhere there is humanity, but especially, it does not belong in Texas, the home of the cowboy in the eyes of the world.

As Winston Churchill once observed, "There is nothing on the inside of a man that cannot be cured by the outside of a horse."

Willie Nelson, Robert Duvall, Larry Hagman, and myself—sometimes known as the Four Horsemen of

KINKY FRIEDMAN

Texas—have vowed to ride against these egregious establishments.

Ride with us, if you will, and visit www.saplonline
.org/horses.htm or www.habitatforhorses.org.

MY PET PROJECT

To those of you who think my career is going to the dogs,
I say: You're right. It's also going to the cats. Because they
need my help. Yours too. It's true, folks. I'm known far
and wide as the Gandhi-like figure of the Utopia Animal
Rescue Ranch. What, you might ask, does a Gandhi-like
figure do? Nothing, of course. And what kind of profit
does this modern-day prophet earn from the daunting
task of doing nothing all the time? None, of course. But if
you keep asking questions, you're going to irritate the
Gandhi-like figure, who has his hands full as the spiritual
leader of sixty-three dogs, twenty-two horses, three don-
keys, nine pigs, two goats, fifteen chickens, eleven cats,
two turkeys, and a rooster named Alfred Hitchcock who
crows precisely at noon.

It all started late in the summer of 1996 at the ungodly hour of seven o'clock as my dog, Mr. Magoo, and I
were driving the campers' dirty laundry into Kerrville
from my family's summer camp, Echo Hill. Some might
find it rather sad that, after fifty years of camping, my
role had devolved to this pathetic, menial task. To me and
Magoo, however, this was an important mission, fraught

I like stray dogs better than fat cats.
(Photo by Rick Reichenbach and Regina Payton)

with many obstacles and challenges, one of which we spotted in the middle of the road that very morning. I slammed on the brakes of the old pickup, leaped sideways out of the cab, and discovered a kitten nestled between the yellow stripes of the highway, roaring like a tiger. The pitiable creature, all of five inches long, was bleeding profusely from a gaping wound in its right front leg.

Certain that the animal was dying, Magoo and I scooped him up and raced him to our friend Bill Hoegemeyer's animal clinic in Kerrville. Dr. Hoegemeyer's diagnosis was that the tiny fellow had been shot by some Great White Hunter. I told him to do whatever it took to save the cat. He amputated the leg, gave the patient two injections during surgery to restart its heart, then gave me a bill for $1,200. I didn't know it then, but Lucky—for that was to become the cat's name—would have a worth that would be virtually incalculable.

In a short period of time, I realized that I'd be on the road too much to adequately provide for the care and feeding of the little convalescing feline patient. So I, for want of a better word, dumped him on Cousin Nancy Parker, a friend of mine who lived in Utopia. In all fairness, Lucky was not the first, nor would he be the last, furry soul I was to deposit on Cousin Nancy's doorstep. I have always felt that what we do when a stray spirit crosses our path—how we react to the hungry, homeless stranger—is indubitably a measure of our own humanity.

In time, Cousin Nancy's little menagerie grew. Soon she had so many animals that she didn't know what to do. Because of this, in 1998 the Utopia Animal Rescue Ranch was born. It was and still is a never-kill sanctuary for stray and abused animals, a court of last resort for those at death's door. But playing God is a role with which Cousin Nancy and I have never felt comfortable. We always knew we could not save every starfish on the sand, only this one.

Today, as before, Cousin Nancy runs the show; her husband, Tony Simons (who can identify each dog by his or her individual bark), is our ranch manager; and I suppose I fall into the category of modern-day Ronald Reagan pitch man. About five years ago, my father, Tom Friedman, in the last year of his life, provided the Rescue Ranch with a new home on the scenic east flat of Echo Hill. Here the animals, in spacious outdoor pens, are cared for by Nancy and Tony, sheltered by the surrounding hills, and protected from a world that, at best, has never been very kind to them. The zip code is Medina, but the ranch is still Utopia. More than anything else, it feels like a peaceful, happy orphanage.

During the eight and a half years of the ranch's existence, many friends and angels have come to our rescue, just as the ranch has come to the rescue of so many animals in distress. My friend John McCall, the Shampoo King from Dripping Springs, has donated more than $50,000. Dwight Yoakam, Don Imus, Jerry Jeff Walker, Robert Earl Keen, Billy Joe Shaver, Jimmie Dale Gilmore, Butch Hancock, Joe Ely, and others too many to mention, have helped us with "bonefits" to raise money for the ranch. Jerry Agiewich has made and distributed a fine line of salsas that has similarly been a financial pleasure. Laura Bush graciously headlined a luncheon for us at the Four Seasons in Austin. She spoke, posed for photographs with everyone, and narrated for the crowd a hilarious slide show depicting animal life in the White House. More recently, the artist Peter Max donated a piece of art, a portrait of the Kinkster with two of the Friedmans, Brownie and Chumley.

What can you do to help? Consider adopting an animal. More than 1,500 Rescue Ranch residents have already been welcomed into loving homes all over the country. (To see photos of the animals up for adoption, go to utopiarescue.com.) Taking in a stray or abused animal can be a life-changing experience, but don't be surprised if your new pet gazes wistfully over his shoulder as you both drive away. Utopia is quite possibly the only home he's known. If you watch carefully, you might even see Cousin Nancy cry.

Of course, she'll always have Lucky. The three-legged cat shares Cousin Nancy and Tony's trailer on the Rescue ranch with twelve dogs, whom he routinely keeps in line with the mere swat of a paw. With the same solitary front paw, he has killed two rattlesnakes. He is, indeed, a very lucky cat. Strong, handsome, and high-spirited, he is a symbol of what a little love can do.

I've always believed that dogs are cowboys and cats are Indians, natural enemies fighting forever across the wide-open prairie of the imagination of a child. Taken together, however, they could well constitute the yin and yang of our souls. It probably wouldn't rain if it weren't for cats and dogs. Their only fault is that they don't live long enough.

Mark Twain once said that when you meet Saint Peter, it's best to leave your dog outside. Heaven, he claimed, runs on protocol. If it ran on merit, your dog would go in and you would stay outside.

While I agree with Twain, I see things a little differently. I believe that when you die and go to heaven, all the dogs and cats you've ever had in your life come running to meet you.

Until that day, rest in peace, dear friends.

I love a parade. Marfa, Texas.
(Photo by Brian Kanof)

8

THOU SHALT NOT EAT A CHICKEN-FRIED STEAK BIGGER THAN YOUR HEAD

OR

Common Sense

George Washington, the man the king of England called the greatest man in the world because he didn't want to be king, never believed in political parties. All we needed in politics and government, he insisted, was "common sense and common honesty." Sadly, these two precious commodities are just as lacking today as they were back in Washington's time. If anything, these qualities are more in demand today than ever before because our government and its leaders are more out of touch with the people. Common sense, it seems, is not all that common these days in the city named after the greatest man in the world.

State governments, which should have been the gatekeepers of American independence, instead have merely become smaller replicas of the mess we find in the nation's capital. In Texas, the results are easy to see. We are second in the production of agricultural products yet we are also second in the number of people in our state who go to bed hungry. For the first time in history, Texas is importing energy. We rank right along the bottom when it comes to funding for children, education, health care, and care for the elderly. As stated earlier, we are first in executions, toll roads, property taxes, and dropouts. Common sense ought to tell us that whatever we're doing just ain't workin'.

WHAT HAS SIX BALLS AND SCREWS TEXANS?

Meanwhile, back in Austin, the state government is busy ignoring all of the above and concentrating instead on matters dealing directly (or indirectly) with power, party, and greed. The state lottery is only one example of this misuse of the public trust. The lottery was designed and sold to the people of Texas as a device for funneling revenues into our much neglected educational system. Indeed, large billboards bedeck practically every highway in the state proclaiming that the lottery has generated $8 billion in eight years for education. The little minor problem we have is that absolutely no one can find any evidence of this money ever actually helping students and teachers. Instead, the money appears to be lining the pockets of the lobbyists and the career politicians.

How do I know this? Some of it is a matter of brazen public record. But if anyone has any doubt about the lottery money never reaching its supposed destination, I offer a tale of two states. Most of us have long ago accepted with quiet desperation the fact that the Texas Lottery has never functioned as advertised. When I tell people my riddle, "What has six balls and screws Texans?" they all laugh because they already know the answer—the Texas Lottery. But the state of Georgia has a lottery too. The only difference is that their lottery money goes to the people and not the politicians. In Georgia, every high school student with a B or better average goes to college free on a full four-year scholarship. In Texas, not one kid goes to college free because of the lottery. Not one teacher or retired teacher has seen a salary increase because of the lottery. How can this be? Why do we let them get away with it?

THE SANTA
ANNA HIGHWAY

Not only does the lottery money go into a "general fund" that gets siphoned off at every level of a vast bureaucracy, but an even bigger boondoggle, the Trans-Texas Corridor, is now being foisted on the people of Texas by the governor and a huge Spanish corporation. ED stands for erectile dysfunction but it also stands for eminent domain, two words that folks in this state will be hearing a lot about if the governor gets his way. Texas's oldest farms, ranches, towns, and churches will be disastrously affected by this monstrous superhighway, often without any remuneration. The budget for this ridiculous adventure may reach $189 billion, and current plans indicate it may go from nowhere to nowhere, with no planned access as of yet to major cities. The Trans-Texas Corridor, or the Santa Anna Highway, as I call it, will take tolls for the next fifty years or more, most of which will go directly to the Spanish corporation. No one knows for sure exactly where the TTC is headed and that's the way the governor and his Spanish cronies like it.

The reelection of Governor Perry virtually assures that big chunks of the land on either side of this monstrosity will be owned by the very same people who own the governor. The plans are secret, the foreign investors and their cohorts are stuffing money in their pants as fast as they can, and it's doubtful at this writing if this abortion will have any effect at all on alleviating congested traffic in and around our major cities. Instead of diligently working to fix education, immigration, energy, and the environment, the governor and his friends are scarring the land forever with this smoke-and-mirrors scam that will benefit no one but the Spanish corporation and their traitorous Texas cohorts. Don't say I didn't warn you.

Common sense is something you're born with. Politicians aren't born; they're hatched like a nefarious scheme. This partly explains why the people who currently run Texas are so far on the wrong side of common sense. If we had initiative and referendum, it would be easy to demonstrate what I've already observed from traversing this great state. The vast majority of the people oppose the Trans-Texas Corridor—I've never met one who didn't.

I'm for the little fellers, not the Rockefellers, and believe me, there are lots more of us than there are of them. But, in order to bring about fundamental change, the little fellers have got to vote. Thus far, they haven't.

THE FIVE MEXICAN
GENERALS PLAN

The politicians talk and talk about immigration, but in Austin and in Washington, they do absolutely nothing. Why is that? It's greed and politics, folks. Poly-ticks. Long before I offered the K.I.S.S.P. program featuring 10,000 National Guard troops on the border, taxpayer ID cards for foreigners who want to work here, and socking it to employers big-time who hire illegals without the new ID cards, I voiced another suggestion to help stem illegal immigration. This was given to me by legendary Texas Ranger Joaquin Jackson. It was called "The Five Mexican Generals Plan." The people laughed when I first sat down at the piano to tell them about "The Five Mexican Generals Plan." They're not laughing now. They realize that no fundamental change in immigration policy is going to be introduced out of Austin or Washington no matter who's in charge. The fact that the Democrats are now running things in the nation's capital merely means that a different swarm of locusts and lobbyists has now descended upon the city. For their own personal, precious, political reasons, nothing will be delivered. I hope I am wrong, but common sense tells me that I'm right.

Therefore, just for the record, let me set down for you the plan Joaquin suggested to me, the plan that everybody thought was a joke but now are not so sure. The Five Mexican Generals Plan goes like this: We divide the border into five jurisdictions and we appoint a Mexican general in charge of each. Then we place a million dollars (or two million, whatever it takes) in a bank account, which we hold in escrow for each general. Then, every time we catch an illegal coming through his section, we withdraw $10,000. This will effectively shut off illegal immigration into Texas.

Last year, George Bush Sr. invited me and Little Jewford to Texas A&M to hear John McCain speak. Afterward, we got a chance to hang out a little with 41 and John McCain. I told them the Five Mexican Generals Plan. The former president chuckled over the plan quite a bit, but Senator McCain's response was quite different. He gave me a sort of wistful smile, then he said, "You know, that Five Mexican Generals Plan is probably better than anything we've got out there right now."

John McCain, of course, was right. It doesn't matter whether or not it's a joke, it merely points out that whatever we're doing (or not doing) now is not working. The plan may be a joke to some, but it's also common sense, the common sense of Joaquin Jackson, a man who knows the border and its problems more than most. Personally, I still strongly advocate the plan. I believe, along with a growing number of others, both inside and outside government, that it's crazy enough to work.

Finally, let me just say that common sense is nothing new in government; it's merely something rare. Thomas Paine, one of the greatest, most significant Americans who ever lived, titled his pamphlet *Common Sense.* On his deathbed, Paine was harassed by clergymen demanding to know his nationality and his religion. Thomas Paine's only response was, "The world is my country; to do good is my religion."

In these troubled times, that's still a damn good answer.

The famous "Gov Bug" designed by Bob Wade. I prefer to call her
"The Hebrew Hummer."
(Photo by Little Jewford)

9

FUCK 'EM IF THEY CAN'T TAKE A JOKE

One of my favorite mantras throughout the campaign, and a credo I still believe in strongly, is that musicians can better run this state than politicians. "We won't get a hell of a lot done in the morning," I said. "But we'll work late—and we'll be honest."

Frankly, *beauticians* could run this state better than politicians. So could opticians, magicians, or morticians. People from outside politics are bound to be a damn sight better at getting the train of Texas back on the track than the ones on the inside who put her in the ditch in the first place.

"We're all passengers on that train," I told the crowds, "and the Good Lord's the engineer. And on November 7, we're gonna get that train of Texas right back on the track!"

As the author Frederick Exley once wrote, "What good are dreams if they come true?" At this writing it's not hard to see that the train is still in the ditch. It's also not hard to see the governor is still out of touch with the people. He still does not know the waitress's name in the coffee shop. I know her name. Sometimes I even ask her for her telephone number.

First as a musician, then as an author, I've traveled all over this great state, and I know that I'm more in touch and in tune with real Texans than most politicians. Think of the last time you were truly inspired by a politician. Think of the last time you really respected one. And think of the last time a politician really respected you.

I've hung out often in my life in rooms full of musicians and now I can also claim—though it's quite far from a brag—that I've also hung out in rooms full of politicians. There's a basic, almost palpable difference between the two groups. The musicians have honesty, integrity, humanity, creativity, and a sense of humor. The politicians, as a general rule, have none of these qualities in any great degree. They lack creative solutions to prob-

100

lems, they are shallow and superficial by their very nature, and they all appear to have had humor bypasses. Whether they are big stars or virtual unknowns, the musicians all seem to evoke a basic sense of decency, a trait noticeably lacking in most politicians.

One of the first people I sought advice from and then tapped to be an integral part of the campaign was Willie Nelson, whom I like to call "The Hillbilly Dalai Lama." For as long as I've known Willie, he's been far to the left of me, not to mention quite a bit higher than me. This was especially true just before the invasion of Iraq when Willie and I were discussing the matter on his bus. To his credit, Willie was against the war from the very beginning. He thought it was a bad idea altogether. I, on the other hand, felt it might be a good idea to knock a dictator off and make the other dictators look over their shoulders a bit.

As we were discussing whether it was a sound plan to invade Iraq, I recall the conversation becoming increasingly animated. Willie, I remember, was smoking a joint about the size of a large kosher salami and I was getting more and more frustrated trying to get through to him. Finally, I said, "Look, Willie. The guy is a tyrannical bully and we've got to take him out!"

"No," said Willie. "He's our president and we've got to stand by him."

CRITICIZE ME
ALL YOU WANT

In late 2004, as I was deciding whether or not to officially throw my hat in the ring, I went to see Willie again to get his blessings and any advice or suggestions he might bestow upon me. He was on the bus writing a new song called "I Hate Every Bone in Your Body Except Mine" and smoking a joint the size of a large cedar fence post.

"Willie," I said, "I've got a great life and, as much as I love Texas, I'm not sure if I want to sacrifice it on the altar of politics. On the other hand, we haven't had an independent candidate even get on the ballot in 154 years and this may be the last opportunity of our lifetime to make this happen."

"And your name is?" Willie said.

After a while we settled down into a discussion of the fact that, for the first time in history, the great state of Texas was importing energy. Willie laid out a highly persuasive argument for bio-diesel and agreed to be my energy czar if the people of Texas had the vision to elect me governor. The fact that Willie has a special rapport with farmers was not lost upon the Kinkster. With Willie in charge, farmer's bio-diesel co-ops would be springing up all over Texas to make bio-diesel readily available to everyone. And, as I went on to often point out in stump speeches all over the state, Willie would be different from the current crop of bureaucrats. He would never have his hand in Texas's pocket.

The more we talked and dreamed, the more we realized that these were two reachable stars—clean energy and clean government. Energy would be Willie's star—fuel you could actually grow. Clean government would be mine—throw the money changers out of the temple. From inside Willie's tour bus we saw what we believed could be a new and beautiful Texas—a Texas that would not be forever following behind but soon would be leading the American parade. It was a wonderful dream, and, like all dreams, we figured, there was a chance it might come true.

Before I left, Willie had even come up with a new campaign slogan for me. It was catchy and clever and would soon be ringing out from Amarillo to Brownsville. It was, "Criticize me all you want, but don't circumcise me anymore."

THE ONLY TWO GOOD
BALLS I EVER HIT

Golf has always been a major love of Willie's life. Willie even shared a story with me about his beloved pastime. It seems that a woman came off of Willie's golf course recently complaining she'd been stung by a bee. The golf pro asked her, "Where'd it sting you?" She responded, "Between the first and second holes." The golf pro said,

"Well, I can tell you right now, your stance is too wide."

Thus it did not surprise me that before the year had passed, I found myself in the midst of a gala golf outing to raise money for the campaign. The fund-raiser gave folks from all over the country the chance to play on Willie's own golf course outside Austin with no less than Willie himself and Jesse Ventura. I was there too, of course, but mostly to meet and greet the people. I don't play golf. The only two good balls I ever hit was when I stepped on the garden rake.

The golf outing raised over a quarter of a million dollars for the campaign, which seemed to us like a lot of money at the time. In politics, of course, it's impossible to calculate accurately, much less honestly, the money that an incumbent might get his greedy hands upon. The best estimate to be made, in retrospect, is that Rick Perry spent more than a hundred times that figure to practically guarantee his reelection. To be sure, we had no idea how high-stakes the game was at the time. We thought a quarter of a million dollars was a lot of money, and it is, outside of politics. It amounts to chump change in politics, unfortunately. It was, however, enough to get the game underway. As Kent Perkins says, "Every journey of a thousand miles begins with a cash advance."

Jesse Ventura, while not a musician himself, admires musicians far more than politicians. He even convinced the late, great Warren Zevon to perform at his inaugural party in Minnesota. Jesse came down to help us several times during the long and winding and tedious road we call the campaign. Dean Barkley was the one who first introduced me to Jesse and I was impressed with the man right from the start. He was the one whom I first heard say, "The guy with the most money shouldn't always win—it's not the American way, it's not the American dream."

As I got to know Jesse better, I realized he was as far from being a politician as you could get; he was a pirate with a heart of gold. For a dreamer, he seemed to me to be a very practical man. For instance, he was against building a fence between Texas and Mexico. "Ten years from now," he said, "*we* might want to get out of *here*."

Yet politics and politicians in this country have amply fulfilled George Washington's worst nightmares. With notable exceptions who are few and far between, I believe most politicians are the crookedest, dirtiest scoundrels in the world. They bribe, extort, bully, lie, and steal on almost a daily basis and they get away with it because all those things are legal in politics. You can't offer a cop a couple hundred bucks when he stops you for a speeding offense. You can't offer your kid's teacher or football coach a bribe. That would be unthinkable. Charges would be brought. The public would be outraged. But in the wonderful world of politics this law-breaking, reprehensible behavior goes on every day. And, as I always like to point out, "The more experience you have, the worse you get." The fact is, most career politicians are better lawbreakers than they are lawmakers.

Why do we, the people, put up with this? Is it some force of nature that men, women, children, and green plants must accept? Not really. It's merely just the house playing with a stacked deck. It's an abuse of power by those in power who should be using that power to help the people. Most politicians soon learn they can get rich off the people, which, of course, they infinitely prefer to simply helping someone. But why have we permitted the politicians to suppress the will of the people for so long in this country? Jesse Ventura has a ready answer for that one. "We are controlled by the Democratic and Republican parties," he says, "which really only gives us one more choice than a dictatorship."

In the waning days of the campaign, our finances were beginning to wane as well. John McCall, the Shampoo King from Dripping Springs, had given us over a million dollars but we had stretched it for almost two years. John claimed he was the only guy who gave bucks and didn't want anything from the candidate. "I didn't even want to talk to Kinky," he told the media. "He'd only ask me for more money." John wanted more than anything else to see a change in Texas politics. As Beano commented, "He put his money where his heart is." John also gave us a big, beautiful campaign headquarters. "I didn't give at the office," he said. "I gave the office."

But people like John are rare birds indeed. Most who give a million or more are merely making an investment. They expect to not only own the candidate, they also expect, and usually get, a good return on their money. That's how the governor of the great state of Texas has become little more than a replaceable implement, owned and controlled by a handful of rich fat cats in Houston and Dallas. Perry can no more act on his own or follow his heart than the man in the moon. And at least the man in the moon comes out once in a while so we can see him. He has nothing to hide.

B O O Z E   I N   T H E
B L E N D E R

Another guy who gave us a real financial boost and didn't want anything for it was Jimmy Buffett. Well, that's almost correct. Jimmy called me out of the blue one day and offered to help and I took him up on it. "If you're elected governor, I only want one thing," he said. "What's that?" I asked. "Port Aransas," he said.

I told this to my friend Rick Reichenbach, who happens to be the lighthouse-keeper in the little coastal town of Port Aransas near Corpus Christi. Rick thought it was a hell of an idea. "If you ceded Port Aransas to Jimmy Buffett for four years," he said, "it'd result in the biggest economic and tourist boom the town has ever seen." I never got a chance to make good on that deal but for his part, Jimmy did.

Jimmy's concert at the Paramount Theater in Austin sold out in about five minutes. Parrotheads flocked in from all over the state and the country. Not only was the show killer bee, the audience colorful as hell, but Jimmy's motivation was that of a musician, not a politician. Political reform and the environment have always been close to his heart in Florida, and I believe these issues moti-

Parrotheads unite! Thank you, Jimmy.
It's been a financial pleasure.
(Photo by Brian Kanof)

vated his involvement in our campaign as well. The Jimmy Buffett concert brought in close to another $250,000.

Philanthropist Carolyn Farb threw several musical events for us at her River Oaks home in Houston, the first featuring Jerry Jeff Walker and Billy Joe Shaver, and the second with Lyle Lovett. At one time or another it seemed like virtually every musician in Texas stepped up to aid our cause. My confidence in the loyalty, decency, and basic generosity of musicians, be they superstars or house bands, was once again renewed. So support your local musician. Like Willie Nelson, he will stay all night and stay a little longer if that's what it takes to satisfy the people.

ON THE ROAD AGAIN

If you traveled in Texas in 2005-2006, you might've noticed any number of vehicles festooned with Kinky bumper stickers, slogans, and designs. Little Joe Hernandez, of Little Joe y la Familia, had his entire large equipment trailer done over in wraparound Kinkster campaign art designed by Austin's great Guy Juke. Pauley Hines's orange and blue Prowler was also bedecked in Kinky style. The third truly outstanding vehicle was designed by the artist Bob Wade and featured a hot-pink trailer with a big black cowboy hat and cigar. It was usually driven around by John Jordan, our director of field operations, or Danni Bonderant, secretary of transportation. I had two great names for this vehicle/art piece but neither was selected by the campaign hierarchy. I wanted to call the little booger "The Party-Crasher" or "The Hebrew Hummer." In their infinite wisdom, the campaign staff decided on "The Gov Bug," claiming that was the choice of supporters on the Internet.

Though I was gracious about this fateful decision going against me, it did hurt. In fact, it hurt more than the night at Scholz's Beer Garten in Austin when I lost the election. By that time I knew that Friedman's just another word for nothing left to lose.

As the votes came in I realized I was not going to have to worry about leaving cigar burns on any of the furniture at the Governor's Mansion. I'd had quite a few Guinnesses by that time and I seemed to be hearing an angel whispering to me in one ear and a devil in the other. Oddly enough, they were both speaking in Willie Nelson's voice. The angel was saying, "Fortunately, we're not in control." The devil was saying, "Fuck 'em if they can't take a joke."

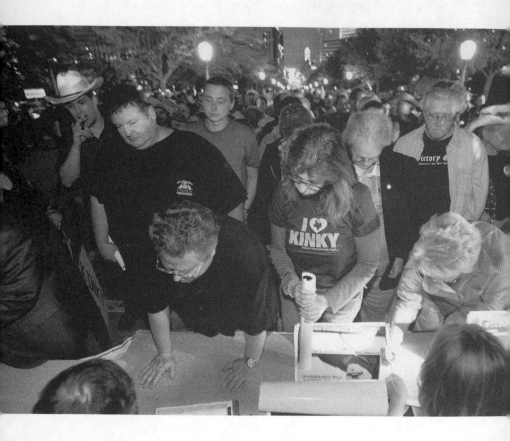

The Austin Tea Party. March 8, 2006, at the stroke of midnight, a ragtag army of patriots and dreamers descend upon the steps of the capitol to sign the petition.

*(Photo by David Woo/*The Dallas Morning News ©*)*

10

ASK NOT IF YOU'RE PROUD OF TEXAS; ASK IF YOU'VE MADE TEXAS PROUD OF YOU

Robert Louis Stevenson once wrote, "It's better to travel hopefully than it is to arrive." Though I did not become governor of Texas, I was able to perform what is perhaps a higher calling. That is, being a dealer in hope. There is no finer thing to do, I believe, than travel this beautiful state, bringing people into the process, some of whom haven't registered or voted in a lifetime, some older folks for whom this seems like a last chance for romance, some young little boogers voting hopefully for the very first time. It was a joyful journey, the hopes and dreams and images of which I shall always treasure.

I saw the campaign headquarters go from a small, shabby room no bigger than your nose, to a vast, sprawling beehive of modern offices filled to overflowing with mostly young people finding meaning in what often seems essentially a meaningless world. What I loved about Jesse Ventura was watching him stand for hours in the hot sun of a university campus discussing matters with small groups of kids, sometimes just one kid. I thought to myself, what politician would you ever see doing this?

Then there was the used car dealer in Hamilton, Texas, who said of yours truly, "If that little shit gets on the ballot, I'm gonna vote for him." And get on the ballot, we did. It was a cold March day and I will never forget that seemingly endless line of young people carrying boxes full of notarized signatures into the secretary of state's office. They were smiling proudly as if they each were carrying The Holy Grail or a newborn babe. It was, indeed, a shining little moment of democracy in action, and if you watched it with a tear in your eye, you were not alone.

I predicted that when, for the first time in 154 years, an independent won the election in Texas, bluebonnets would be springing up all over America. That, sadly, did not happen. We did receive more than half a million votes, enough to have won in many states. Unfortunately, sometimes, everything *is* bigger in Texas. The pundits, the parties, the pollsters, the politicians, and in some cases the media itself, all warned the voter about "wasting your vote."

I responded that if you vote your heart, if you vote your conscience, if you vote your dreams, you never waste your vote.

Stated quite simply, voter apathy was the windmill we could not beat. During the entire course of this sally into establishment politics, we won almost every single poll that was conducted outside the small universe of likely voters. Virtually every high school mock election, virtually every newspaper, radio, or television poll, virtually every straw poll of any nature, we ran away with, as long as it wasn't screened and weighted and sifted for only the usual pool of voters. In a situation like this, it is invariably the few who control the destinies of the many. The politicians know this and they like to keep it this way. They, along with the sometimes seemingly complicit media, use likely voter polls as clubs, trumpeting them all over the news, to show people that it doesn't pay to vote. They know that if people don't think somebody can win, they won't vote for him, or even more likely, they just won't vote at all.

THE GOOD SHEPHERD

I always said this would not be a political campaign; it would be a spiritual quest, a search for the soul of Texas. And so it was. As a Judeo-Christian, I've always had Jesus and Moses in my heart, two good Jewish boys who got in a little trouble with the government. As the campaign rolled, I added other personal heroes of mine to my stump speeches: Gandhi, Martin Luther King, and Fathe

Damien. Every one of these five great men died broke—
they didn't have $100 million to blow on an election, nor
would they have—and yet, they will live forever. There is
something more important than political correctness and
that is moral correctness. Not overbearing, politically
tinged morality, but moral responsibility, as Ronald Reagan described it; the responsibility to help those less for-
tunate than us who, through no fault of their own, find
themselves needing our aid and compassion. Remember,
we need to help the little fellers, not the Rockefellers.

It was only months before election day when I lost
another vote, as my old friend Bill Hardin died in Kerrville.
Bill's funeral was at the Presbyterian church where the
minister, Rob Lohmeyer, read from the New Testament
about the Good Shepherd. As a Jew, I had never really read
the New Testament. (I had, of course, never really read the
Old Testament either.) But the passages about the Good
Shepherd made for some peaceful sailing in my heart.

The minister told of how, at the end of the day, all
the shepherds and their flocks mingled together by the
river. But the Good Shepherd, he said, knows and recog-
nizes his own, and his own know and recognize him. Boy,
I thought, there's hardly a politician alive whom you
could honestly say that about. And the longer they're in,
the more out-of-touch they become. Of all people, a career politician is among the least likely to know and recognize his own. Similarly, voters may know his name, but
they can rarely be said to really know and recognize him.

"And when the wolves come," read the minister, "the
~ed hand flees. But the Good Shepherd stays." Bill

Hardin was already a precious passenger on the train to glory, but I could not get that last passage out of my head or my heart. That was a perfect description of most politicians, I thought. They were hired hands. That was why we didn't need a politician for a governor anymore. What we really needed was a Good Shepherd. Predictably, perhaps, the politicians didn't quite see it this way.

But the Good Shepherd did resonate with the people I consider to comprise the very heart of Texas, many of them young people. I told these young little boogers that if they were old enough to fight in Iraq, they were old enough to help us fix Texas. "Martin Luther King is not a street!" I reminded them every chance I got. "JFK is not an airport! And Ronnie Reagan's not an airport either! And Cesár Chávez is not a street! They were flesh-and-blood people just like us, except they dreamed a little bigger than most people and they knew the cavalry wasn't coming to save us. Whatever we do, we've got to do it ourselves, right here in Texas. So ask not if you're proud of Texas; ask if you've made Texas proud of you."

YOUNG VOICES

Some of the youth energized by our campaign were very young indeed. My true feelings, in fact, regarding my recent foray into politics were probably best expressed by child. The child's name is Natalie, the seven-year- daughter of Kay and Brad Wicall, owners of Bradz S in Austin. Though Kay is a hairstylist, for most of the past year she had taken leave from her work to be chief fund-raiser for our campaign. It wasn't unusual for us to have her as our fund-raiser. Like I said, everyone on the staff seemed to be either a hairdresser or a bass player. No politicians or lobbyists allowed. That having been said, Kay, like many, many others, had put all of her considerable heart and soul into this spiritual adventure.

On the morning after the election, when Kay woke Natalie, the second-grader opened her eyes and said, "I'm sorry Kinky lost, Mom."

This caused one stubborn tear to roll slowly down Kay's cheek. Natalie looked at her mother for a moment. Then she spoke again.

"But aren't you glad you played the game?" she said.

I HAVE A DREAM

It was a long road trip late in the campaign—Austin, Waco, Dallas, Fort Worth, Amarillo, Midland, and Odessa—all within one twenty-four hour period. We drove some and flew some, and every truck stop and airport seemed full of enthusiastic supporters. We'd come a long way from early in the race at the Texas State Fair in Dallas when I met a pig farmer who uttered these immortal words: "Kinky, ou may not be worth a damn, but you're better'n what ve got."

Somewhere between Austin and Amarillo, with Lit-

tle Jewford at the wheel, I nodded out. I've always been a bit concerned about nodding out as a passenger in a moving vehicle, because I did not relish the possibility of waking up in hell. Jewford assured me, however, that that would be no problem. He had a townhouse in hell, he claimed. Maybe hell was on my mind, because that's what I dreamed about. But in the dream, I wasn't going to hell. Rick Perry was.

I dreamed that Rick Perry passed away and went up to see Saint Peter. "Get out of my way," Perry tells him, "I'm comin' through." "Hold the weddin', Governor," says Saint Peter. "We have a little different way of doing things up here. First you'll spend twenty-four hours in hell, then you'll spend twenty-four hours in heaven. Then we'll let you decide."

So Perry goes down, down, down to hell in the elevator and when the doors open he's on a beautiful golf course. All his cohorts and lobbyists are there, drinking champagne and laughing and having a lot of fun. The devil's there too, and he's a great guy, joking and dancing around. So Perry joins all his friends and they spend the day telling stories about all the insider deals they made and laughing about all the money they made off the backs of the people.

Finally, the twenty-four hours are up and Perry goes up to heaven, where he spends the next twenty-four hours walking on clouds with angels, which isn't too bad either. Then Saint Peter comes up to Perry.

"Okay, Governor," he says, "you've spent twenty-four hours in heaven and twenty-four hours in hell. Now, it's your turn to decide. Where will you spend all eternity?"

"You know," said Perry, "I never thought I'd say this, but I think I'd rather be in hell."

So down, down, down the elevator goes, but when the doors open, Perry sees that the golf course is gone. In its place is a barren field covered with trash, and all of Perry's friends are dressed in rags, looking miserable, picking up the trash and putting it in bags.

"What's going on?" shouted Perry in total bewilderment. "What happened?"

Then the devil put his arm around Perry's shoulder and he smiled. "Yesterday, Governor," he said, "we were campaigning. Today, you voted."

BIRD IN THE HAND

There came a time on the night of the election when Bill Hillsman came up to me and suggested that I should address the crowd at Scholz's Beer Garten. The crowd was huge and I wasn't sure what to tell them. Bill said things did not look good for us but not to concede yet. Nevertheless, he felt, the people needed to hear from the candidate. I needed to tell them something that would give them hope.

One of the great challenges for a dealer in hope is to continue to distribute that dear commodity when almost all is lost. Besides, these were the sons and daughters of Texas who had fought in the trenches, not for party or power or greed but for the Alamo of the mind. These were the people who had fought for Texas itself.

I'm not sure if the crowd realized that Little Jewford, wearing his sparkling jacket that looked like Elvis's shower curtain, for once in his life did not introduce me as "the next governor of the great state of Texas." He too knew it was just about over. But somehow the crowd sounded more like a victory celebration was taking place. They still believed and I hope they always will.

I had a victory speech in my mind and I had a concession speech of sorts, but I had no idea what I was going to say to them now. I thought of what Willie Nelson told me: Never give 'em everything you've got. I didn't want to give 'em everything I had. It was too sad. I also thought of what Robert Louis Stevenson once wrote, "It's a far better thing that the lad should break his neck, than that you should break his spirit." They had plenty of spirit. And I wasn't going to break it.

So I began by thanking the campaign staff for doing a great job. Angels could do no more, I told them. Then I thanked all the volunteers, who had been the brick and mortar of what was truly a spiritual quest. Perhaps it was all the young people in the crowd that started me thinking of my dad, whom the kids all called Uncle Tom, telling stories around the campfire at Echo Hill, our family's summer camp. One of the stories Tom told every year seemed to fit the moment, so I decided to borrow it. I knew he wouldn't have minded.

There once was a great Indian chief, I told the crowd, and a small group of young bucks who wished to topple him from power. One of them came up with a clever idea, which he would spring on the chief that night at the big campfire in front of the whole tribe. When the time came to ask the wise old chief questions, the young buck would hold a small bird in his closed fist. The question for the chief would be, Is the bird living or is it dead? If the chief said the bird was alive, he would squeeze his fist and then show everyone that it was dead. If the chief said the bird was dead, he would merely open his hand and the bird would fly away. Either way, the chief would look like a fool in front of the tribe.

When the time came that night at the big campfire, the young buck stood up, holding up the bird in his closed fist. "O great, wise chief," he said, "in my hand I hold a small bird. Is this bird living or is it dead?"

The chief looked at the young buck, and then he spoke. "You say you have a small bird in your hand. You ask, is this bird living or is it dead? I will answer your question. Whether the bird is living or dead, my son, depends on you."

And that little bird represents the hope that we, the people, will someday triumph over this corrupt system of career politicians practicing their politics as usual. Whether the bird flies or dies, my friends, depends on us.

A TRUTH-SEEKING MISSILE: A TRIBUTE TO MOLLY IVINS

A true maverick died in Texas as I was finishing this book, and they don't make 'em extra.

There'll always be plenty of George Bushs and John

The candidate, moments after supposedly losing the election. "To those who feel, life's a tragedy. To those who think, a comedy."
(Photo by David Woo/The Dallas Morning News ©)

Kerrys to go around; the Crips and the Bloods will trot them out every four years whether we like it or not. But a voice in the wilderness, like the still, small voice within, is a song to be savored while we have it, whether we're listening or not, and when we have lost it, we should mourn for ourselves. Such a voice was that of Molly Ivins.

I met her on the gangplank of Noah's Ark. I did not agree with her on a lot of things. Like Frank Sinatra, I've gotten more conservative as I've gotten older. But not Molly. With the awkward grace of a child of our times, she clung to her ideals and notions and hopes, riding forever against the wind in a state as red as the blood of a dying cowboy. The word I'm looking for is "righteous." Righteous without being self-righteous.

Molly was a truth-seeking missile. She was a devil and an angel and a spiritual chop-buster who went after anybody who got in the way of a better world. Quite often she towered above the people she wrote about. They, as likely as not, were merely the slick, lubricated heads of well-oiled political machines; she was a dreamer, a little girl lost at the county fair, who somehow grew up to be a brave and bawdy and brilliant ballbuster in a state where men have always been men and emus have always been nervous.

In an age in which the five major religions are Bank of America, Wal-Mart, McDonald's, Kentucky Fried Chicken, and Starbucks, Molly Ivins was an atheist. The *New York Times*, which got Herman Melville's name wrong in his obituary, called Molly a "liberal newspaper columnist." The *L.A. Times* said she was a "political humorist and best-selling author." They were right, of course, but those are the words we use when we don't know what to say.

In her dark, American heart, Molly was mostly a troublemaker with the feisty spirit of Jesus Christ, John Brown, Joe Hill, and, not to be a male chauvinist or needlessly alliterative, Joan of Arc and Josephine Baker. Two, and possibly three, among this esteemed and reviled assemblage spent time in France. Molly studied in Paris. I do not like France. I do not know what Molly thought of that country. I know she loved this one.

It is, however, the sacred duty of the troublemaker to stir the putrid pot of humanity every now and again, to make people see that there is something more important than political correctness, and that is moral correctness, and to challenge the prayers and the promises of the heartbroken land she loved. And she did it mostly with wit and humor, the kind of humor that sailed dangerously close to the truth without sinking the ship. There are two kinds of sailors, they say; the sailor who fights the sea and the sailor who loves the sea. Molly loved the sea.

I loved Molly because she would say things nobody else had the *cojones* to say, always in a funny and charming Texas way, of course. Imagine a big, brazen cowgirl walking up and saying, "That boy's jeans are on so tight, if he farted he'd blow his boots off."

My dad, Tom, was a World War II hero, and Molly had long been one of *his* heroes, though he had never met her. After he had a heart attack, Molly showed up on our doorstep one afternoon just to visit with him. Molly lifted Tom's spirits immensely and her gesture touched him deeply, as it did his son.

Finally, Molly gave me the greatest slogan I had in my recent campaign for governor of Texas. The slogan was, "Why the hell not?" Why the hell not, indeed. In this homogenized, trivialized, sanitized world, she stands as a lighthouse not just to the left but to us all. Peace be with you, Molly.

ACKNOWLEDGMENTS

The author would like to thank all the usual suspects who helped with the preparation, irritation, and documentation involved with this book. They are, in a random and haphazard order: Max Swafford, Billy Joe Shaver, Debora Hanson, Laura Stromberg, Jean Spain, Brian Kanof, Mark Shurley, David Vigliano, agent; Nancy Parker Simons, Rev. Goat Carson, David Rosenthal, Nina Schwartz, editors; Little Jewford, and Lieutenant Governor Chicken Dick. Several stories in this book have previously appeared, in various forms, in *Texas Monthly* magazine.